AN INTRODUCTION TO

THE PHILOSOPHY OF LAW

Based on the Storrs Lectures
delivered at Yale University

AN INTRODUCTION TO

THE PHILOSOPHY OF LAW

BY ROSCOE POUND

NEW HAVEN · YALE UNIVERSITY PRESS

*To Joseph Henry Beale
in grateful acknowledgment of many obligations*

Preface to First Edition

THIS book is a written version of lectures delivered before the Law School of Yale University as Storrs Lectures in the school year 1921–22.

A metaphysician who had written on the secret of Hegel was congratulated upon his success in keeping the secret. One who essays an introduction to the philosophy of law may easily achieve a like success. His hearers are not unlikely to find that he has presented not one subject but two, presupposing a knowledge of one and giving them but scant acquaintance with the other. If he is a philosopher, he is not unlikely to have tried a highly organized philosophical apparatus upon those fragments of law that lie upon the surface of the legal order or upon the law as seen through the spectacles of some jurist who had interpreted it in terms of a wholly different philosophical system. Looking at the list of authorities relied upon in Spencer's *Justice*, and noting that his historical legal data were taken from Maine's *Ancient Law* and thus came shaped by the political-idealistic interpretation of the English historical school, it is not difficult to perceive why positivist and Hegelian came to the same juristic results by radically different methods. On the other hand, if he is a lawyer he will very likely have been able to do no more than attempt none too intelligently to work with the complicated and delicate engines of others upon the toughest and most resistant of legal materials. Until some Anglo-American jurist arises with the universal equipment of Josef Kohler the results of common-law incursions into philosophy will resemble the effort of the editorial writer who wrote upon Chinese metaphysics after reading in the *Encyclopædia Britannica* under China and metaphysics and combining his information. Yet such incursions there must be. Philosophy has been a powerful instrument in the legal armory and the times are ripe for restoring it to its old place therein. At least one may show what philosophy has done for some of the chief problems of the science of law, what stands before us to be done in some of the more conspicuous problems of that science today in which philosophy may help us, and how it is possible to look at these problems philosophically without treating them in terms of the eighteenth-century natural law or the nineteenth-century metaphysical jurisprudence which stand for philosophy in the general understanding of lawyers .

Roscoe Pound

Harvard Law School,
October 25, 1921

Preface to Revised Edition

PROBLEMS of philosophy of law have arisen in the generation since the first edition which have required rethinking of some of the things I said in 1921–22. Likewise discussions and recent theories of legal liability and some features of the law of property and of the law of contract, which have been developed throughout the world in recent decades, have called not only for rewriting of no little but also for considerable additions to the original text. The bibliography has been rewritten and added to to bring it reasonably down to date.

ROSCOE POUND

University of California at Los Angeles,
Law School,
January 26, 1953

Contents

The Function of Legal Philosophy

FOR twenty-four hundred years—from the Greek thinkers of the fifth century B.C. who asked whether right was right by nature or only by enactment and convention, to the social philosophers of today, who seek the ends, the ethical basis and the enduring principles of social control—the philosophy of law has taken a leading role in all study of human institutions. The perennial struggle of American administrative law with nineteenth-century constitutional formulations of Aristotle's threefold classification of governmental power, the stone wall of natural rights against which attempts to put an end to private war in industrial disputes for a long time dashed in vain, and the notion of a logically derivable superconstitution, of which actual written constitutions are faint and imperfect reflections, which was a clog upon social legislation in the nineteenth and the first decade of the present century, long bore witness how thoroughly the philosophical legal thinking of the past is a force in the administration of justice of the present. Indeed the everyday work of the courts was never more completely shaped by abstract philosophical ideas than in the nineteenth century when lawyers affected to despise philosophy and analytical jurists believed they had set up a self-sufficient science of law which stood in no need of any philosophical apparatus.

In all stages of what may be described fairly as legal development philosophy has been a useful servant. But in some it has been a tyrannous servant and in all but form a master.

It has been used to break down the authority of outworn tradition, to bend authoritatively imposed rules that admitted of no change to new uses which changed profoundly their practical effect, to bring new elements into the law from without and make new bodies of law from these new materials, to organize and systematize existing legal materials and to fortify established rules and institutions when periods of growth were succeeded by periods of stability and of merely formal reconstruction. Such have been its actual achievements. Yet all the while its professed aim has been much more ambitious. It has sought to give us a complete and final picture of social control. It has sought to lay down a moral and legal and political chart for all time. It has had faith that it could find the everlasting, unchangeable legal reality in which we might rest, and could enable us to establish a perfect law by which human relations might be ordered forever without uncertainty and freed from need of change. Nor may we scoff at this ambitious aim and this lofty faith. They have been not the least factors in the power of legal philosophy to do the less ambitious things which in their aggregate are the bone and sinew of legal achievement. For the attempt at the larger program has led philosophy of law incidentally to do the things that were immediately and practically serviceable, and the doing of these latter, as it were *sub specie aeternitatis*, has given enduring worth to what seemed but by-products of philosophical inquiry.

Two needs have determined philosophical thinking about law. On the one hand, the paramount social interest in the general security, which as an interest in peace and order dictated the very beginnings of law, has led men to seek some fixed basis of a certain ordering of human action which should restrain magisterial as well as individual willfulness and assure a firm and stable social order. On the other hand, the pressure of less immediate social interests, and the need of reconciling them with the exigencies of the general security and of making continual new compromises because of continual changes in society have called ever for readjustment at least of the details of the social order. They have called continually for overhauling of legal precepts and for refitting them to unexpected situations. And this has led men to seek principles of legal development by which to escape from authoritative rules which they feared or did not know how to reject but could no longer apply to advantage. These principles of change and growth, however, might easily prove inimical to the general security, and it was important to reconcile or unify them with the idea of a fixed basis of the legal order. Thus the philosopher has sought to construct theories of law and theories of lawmaking and has sought to unify them by some ultimate solving idea equal to the task of yielding a perfect law which should stand fast forever. From the time when lawgivers gave over the attempt to maintain the general security by belief that particular bodies of human law had been divinely dictated or divinely revealed or divinely sanctioned, they have had to wrestle with the problem of proving to mankind that the law was something fixed and settled, whose authority was beyond question, while at the same time enabling it to make constant readjustments and occasional radical changes under the pressure of infinite and variable human desires. The philosopher has worked upon this problem with the materials of the actual legal systems of the time and place or with the legal materials of the past upon which his generation had built. Hence in closer view philosophies of law have been attempts to give a rational account of the law of the time and place, or attempts to formulate a general theory of the legal order to meet the needs of some given period of legal development, or attempts to state the results of the two former attempts universally and to make them all-sufficient for law every-

where and for all time. Historians of the philosophy of
law have fixed their eyes chiefly on the third. But this
is the least valuable part of legal philosophy. If we look
at the philosophies of the past with our eyes upon the law
of the time and place and the exigencies of the stage of legal
development in which they were formulated, we shall be
able to appreciate them more justly, and so far as the law of
the time and place or the stage of legal development was
similar to or different from the present to utilize them for the
purposes of today.

We know Greek law from the beginnings of a legal order
as pictured in the Homeric poems to the developed commercial institutions of the Hellenistic period. In its first stage
the kings decide particular causes by divine inspiration. In
a second stage the customary course of decision has become a
tradition possessed by an oligarchy. Later, popular demand
for publication results in a body of enactment. At first enactments are no more than declaratory. But it was an easy
step from publication of established custom to publication
of changes as if they were established custom and thus to
conscious and avowed changes and intentional new rules
through legislation. The law of Athens in the fifth and fourth
centuries B.C. was a codified tradition eked out by legislation
and individualized in its application through administration
of justice by large popular assemblies. Thus in spite of
formal reduction to writing it preserved the fluidity of
primitive law and was able to afford a philosophy for Roman
law in its stage of equity and natural law—another period of
legal fluidity. The development of a strict law out of codified
primitive materials, which in Rome happily preceded the
stage of equity and natural law, did not take place in the
Greek city. Hence the rules of law were applied with an
individualized equity that reminds us of the French *droit
coutumier*—a mode of application which, with all its good

points, must be preceded by a body of strict law, well worked out and well understood, if its results are to be compatible with the general security in a complex social order. In Athens of the classical period the word νόμος, meaning both custom and enacted law as well as law in general, reflected the uncertainty with respect to form and the want of uniformity in application, which are characteristic of primitive law, and invited thought as to the reality behind such confusion.

We may understand the materials upon which Greek philosophers were working if we look at an exhortation addressed by Demosthenes to an Athenian jury. Men ought to obey the law, he said, for four reasons: because laws were prescribed by God, because they were a tradition taught by wise men who knew the good old customs, because they were deductions from an eternal and immutable moral code, and because they were agreements of men with each other binding them because of a moral duty to keep their promises. It was not long since that men had thought of legal precepts as divinely revealed, nor was it long since that law had been a tradition of old customs of decision. Philosophers were seeking a better basis for them in eternal principles of right. In the meantime in political theory, at least, many of them were the agreements of Athenian citizens as to how they should conduct themselves in the inevitable clashes of interests in everyday life. What was needed above all was some theory of the authority of law which should impose bonds of reason upon those who enacted, upon those who applied, and upon those who were subject to law in such an amorphous legal order.

A sure basis of authority resting upon something more stable than human will and the power of those who govern to impose their will for the time being was required also for the problem of social control in the Greek city-state. In order to maintain the general security and the security of social institutions amid a strife of factions in a society organized on the basis of kinship and against the willfulness of masterful individuals boasting descent from gods, in order to persuade or coerce both the aristocracy and the mass of the low born to maintain in orderly fashion the social *status quo*, it would not do to tell them that law was a gift of God, nor that what offended the aristocrat as a radical bit of popular legislation enacted at the instance of a demagogue was yet to be obeyed because it had been so taught by wise men who knew the good old customs, nor that Demos chafing under some item of a class-possessed tradition was bound by it as something to which all citizens had agreed. The exigencies of the social order called for a distinction between νόμος and τὰ νομιζόμενα —between law and rules of law. The *Minos*, which if not actually a dialogue of Plato's seems clearly Platonic and very close to Plato in time, is taken up with this distinction and gives us a clue to the juristic problems of the time.

Another example may be seen in Aristotle's well-known discussion in the *Nicomachean Ethics*. It is significant that Greek thinkers always couple custom and enactment; things which today we contrast. These were the formal bases of legal authority. So Aristotle considers, not natural *law* and positive *law*, but what is just in itself—just by nature or just in its idea—and what derives its sole title to be just from convention or enactment. The latter, he says, can be just only with respect to those things which by nature are in-different. Thus when a newly reconstituted city took a living Spartan general for its eponymus, no one was bound by na-ture to sacrifice to Brasidas as to an ancestor, but he was bound by enactment and after all the matter was one of convention which, in a society framed on the model of an organized kindred, required that the citizens have a common heroic ancestor, and was morally indifferent. The distinction was handed down to modern legal science by Thomas

Aquinas, was embodied in Anglo-American legal thought by Blackstone, and has become staple. But it is quite out of its setting as a doctrine of *mala prohibita* and *mala in se*. An example of the distinction between law and rules of law has become the basis of an arbitrary line between the traditionally antisocial, penalized by the common law, and recently penalized infringements of newly or partially recognized social interests. Although the discrimination between what is just and right by nature and what is just because of custom or enactment has had a long and fruitful history in philosophical jurisprudence and is still a force in the administration of justice, I suspect that the permanent contribution of Greek philosophy of law is to be found rather in the distinction between law and rules of law, which lies behind it and has significance for all stages of legal development.

Roman lawyers came in contact with philosophy in the transition from the strict law to the stage of equity and natural law, and the contact had much to do with enabling them to make the transition. From a purely legal standpoint Greek law was in the stage of primitive law. Law and morals were still largely undifferentiated. Hence Greek philosophical thinking of a stage of undifferentiated law and morals lent itself to the identification of the legal and the moral in juristic thinking which was characteristic of the classical Roman law. But the strict law obviously was indifferent to morals and in many vital points was quite at variance with the moral ideas of the time. The Greek distinction of just by nature and just by convention or enactment was suggested at once by such a situation. Moreover the forms of law at the end of the Republic and at the beginning of the Empire invited a theory of law as something composite, made up of more than one type of precept and resting immediately on more than one basis of authority.

Cicero enumerates seven forms of law. Three of these are

not heard of thereafter in Roman juristic writing. Evidently already in Cicero's time they belonged to the past and had ceased to be effective forms of actual law. The four remaining, namely, statutes, resolutions of the senate, edicts of the magistrates, and the authority of those learned in the law, come to three—legislation, administrative edicts, and juristic reasoning on the basis of the legal tradition. And these correspond to the three elements which made up the law. First, there was the *ius ciuile:* the Twelve Tables, subsequent legislation, interpretation of both, and the traditional law of the city. Second, there was the mass of rules, in form largely procedural, which was contained in the edicts. The growing point of the law had been here and to some extent growth was still going on through this means. Indeed this part of the law reached its final form under Hadrian. Third, there were the writings of the jurisconsults. The growing point of the law had begun to be here and this was the most important form of law in the classical period from Augustus to the third century. This part of the law got its final form in the *Digest* of Justinian. Of the three elements the first was thought of originally as declared and published custom. Later it was thought of as resting on the authority of the state. It was obviously local and peculiar to Rome. In form it rested on the legislative power of the Roman people, supplemented by a mere interpretation of the legislative command with only the authority of customary acceptance. In Greek phrase it rested on convention and enactment. The second purported to be the rules observed by civilized peoples, and on points of commercial law may well have been an approximation thereto. Apart from this, however, according to ancient ideas of personal law, the rules which obtained among civilized peoples were eminently a proper law to apply between citizen and noncitizen. In Greek phrase it was law by convention. The basis of the third was simply reason. The jurisconsult had no legislative power and no *imperium*. The authority of his *responsum*, as soon as law ceased to be a class tradition, was to be found in its intrinsic reasonableness; in the appeal which it made to the reason and sense of justice of the *iudex*. In Greek phrase, if it was law it was law by nature.

As the rise of professional lawyers, the shifting of the growing point of law to juristic writing, and the transition from the law of a city to a law of the world called for a legal science, there was need of a theory of what law was that could give a rational account of the threefold body of rules in point of origin and authority, which were actually in operation, and would at the same time enable the jurists to shape the existing body of legal precepts by reason so as to make it possible for them to serve as law for the whole world. The perennial problem of preserving stability and admitting of change was presented in an acute form. Above all, the period from Augustus to the second quarter of the third century was one of growth. But it was revolutionary only if we compare the law at the end of the period with the law of the generation before Cicero. The jurisconsults were practical lawyers and the paramount interest in the general security was ever before their eyes. While as an ideal they identified law with morals they did not cease to observe the strict law where it was applicable nor to develop its precepts by analogy according to the known traditional technique when new phases of old questions came before them. Hence what to the Greeks was a distinction between right by nature and right by convention or enactment became to them a distinction between law by nature and law by custom or legislation. The Latin equivalent of τὸ δίκαιον (the right or the just) became their word for law. They said *ius* where Cicero said *lex*. And this convenient ambiguity, lending itself to identification of what ought to be and what is, gave a scientific foundation for the belief of the jurisconsults that when and where they were not bound by positive law they had but to expound the reason and justice of the thing in order to lay down the law.

It must be borne in mind that "nature" did not mean to antiquity what it means to us who are under the influence of the idea of evolution. To the Greek, it has been said, the natural apple was not the wild one from which our cultivated apple has been grown, but rather the golden apple of the Hesperides. The "natural" object was that which expressed most completely the idea of the thing. It was the perfect object. Hence the natural law was that which expressed perfectly the idea of law, and a rule of natural law was one which expressed perfectly the idea of law applied to the subject in question; the one which gave to that subject its perfect development. For legal purposes reality was to be found in this ideal, perfect, natural law, and its organ was juristic reason. Legislation and the edict, so far as they had any more than a positive foundation of political authority, were but imperfect and ephemeral copies of this jural reality. Thus the jurists came to the doctrine of the *ratio legis*, the principle of natural law behind the legal rule, which has been so fruitful both of practical good and of theoretical confusion in interpretation. Thus also they came to the doctrine of reasoning from the analogy of all legal rules, whether traditional or legislative, since all, so far as they had jural reality, had it because and to the extent that they embodied or realized a principle of natural law.

Natural law was a philosophical theory for a period of growth. It arose to meet the exigencies of the stage of equity and natural law, one of the great creative periods of legal history. Yet, as we have seen, even the most rapid growth does not permit the lawyer to ignore the demand for stability. The theory of natural law was worked out as a means of growth, as a means of making a law of the world on the basis of the old strict law of the Roman city. But it was worked out also as a means of directing and organizing the growth of law so as to maintain the general security. It was the task of the jurists to build and shape the law on the basis of the old local materials so as to make it an instrument for satisfying the wants of a whole world while at the same time insuring uniformity and predicability. They did this by applying a new but known technique to the old materials. The technique was one of legal reason; but it was a legal reason identified with natural reason and worked out and applied under the influence of a philosophical ideal. The conception of natural law as something of which all positive law was but declaratory, as something by which actual rules were to be measured, to which so far as possible they were to be made to conform, by which new rules were to be framed, and by which old rules were to be extended or restricted in their application was a powerful instrument in the hands of the jurists and enabled them to proceed in their task of legal construction with assured confidence.

But the juristic empiricism by which the *ius ciuile* was made into a law of the world needed something more than a theoretical incentive. It was a process of analogical development by extension here and restriction there, of generalization, first in the form of maxims and later by laying down broad principles, and of cautious striking out of new paths, giving them course and direction by trial and error. It was a process very like that by which Anglo-American judicial empiricism has been able to make a law of the world on the basis of the legal precepts of seventeenth-century England. Such a process required something to give direction to juristic reasoning, to give definite content to the ideal, to provide a reasonably defined channel for juristic thought. This need was met by the philosophical theory of the nature of things and of the law of nature as conformity thereto. In practice

jurist-made and judge-made law have been molded consciously or unconsciously by ideas as to what law is for; by
theories as to the end of law. In the beginnings of law men
had no more ambitious conception than a peaceable ordering
of society at any cost. But the Greeks soon got a better conception of an orderly and peaceable maintaining of the social
status quo. When the theory of natural law is applied to
that conception, we get the notion of an ideal form of the
social *status quo*—a form which expresses its nature, a perfect
form of the social organization of a given civilization—as
that which the legal order is to further and maintain. Thus
judge and jurist obtain a guide which has served them well
ever since. They are to measure all situations by an idealized
form of the social order of the time and place and are so to
shape the law as to make it maintain and further this ideal
of the social *status quo*. We shall meet this idea in various
forms throughout the subsequent history of the philosophy
of law. It constitutes the permanent contribution of Rome
to legal philosophy.

As soon as scientific legal development begins in the Middle Ages the law once more comes in contact with philosophy
through the study of both in the universities. What was the
need of the time which philosophy was called upon to
satisfy? Following an era of anarchy and disunion and violence men desired order and organization and peace. They
called for a philosophy that would bolster up authority and
rationalize their desire to impose a legal yoke upon society.
The period was one of transition from the primitive law of
the Germanic peoples to a strict law, through reception of
Roman law as authoritative legislation or through compila-
tion of the Germanic customary law more or less after the
Roman model, as in the north of France, or through declaration of the customary law in reported decisions of strong
central courts, as in England. Thus it soon became a period

of strict law. Scholastic philosophy, with its reliance upon dialectic development of authoritatively given premises, its faith in formal logic, and its central problem of putting reason as a foundation under authority, responded exactly to these demands. It is no misnomer to style the commentators or post-glossators of the fourteenth and fifteenth centuries the "scholastic jurists." For it was in large part the philosophy that met the needs of the time so completely which enabled them to put the Roman law of Justinian in a form to be received and administered in the Europe of nine centuries later. While they made the gloss into law in place of the text and made many things over, as they had to be made over if they were to fit a wholly different social order, the method of dialectical development of absolute and unquestioned premises made it appear that nothing had been done but to develop the logical implications of an authoritative text. Men could receive the law of Bartolus so long as they believed it but the logical unfolding of the pre-existing content of the binding legislation of Justinian. It is interesting to note in Fortescue an application of this to the rules of the common law in its stage of strict law. He assumes that these rules are the principles of which he reads in the commentators on Aristotle and that they may be compared to the axioms of the geometrician. The time had not yet come to call rules or principles or axioms in question. The need was to rationalize men's desire to be governed by fixed rules and to reconcile, in appearance at least, the change and growth which are inevitable in all law with the need men felt of having a fixed, unchangeable, authoritative rule. The scholastic philosophy did notable service in these respects and, I venture to think, left as a permanent contribution to legal science the method of insuring certainty by logical development of the content of authoritatively defined conceptions.

On the breakdown of the feudal social organization, the

rise of commerce and the era of discovery, colonization, and exploitation of the natural resources of new continents, together with the rise of nations in place of loose congeries of vassal-held territories, called for a national law unified within the national domain. Starkey proposed codification to Henry VIII and Dumoulin urged harmonizing and unifying of French customary law with eventual codification. The Protestant jurist-theologians of the sixteenth century found a philosophical basis for satisfying these desires of the time in the divinely ordained state and in a natural law divorced from theology and resting solely upon reason, reflecting the boundless faith in reason which came in with the Renaissance. Thus each national jurist might work out his own interpretation of natural law by dint of his own reason, as each Christian might interpret the word of God for himself as his own reason and conscience showed the way. On the other hand, the Catholic jurists of the Counter-Reformation found a philosophical basis for satisfying these same desires in a conception of natural law as a system of limitations on human action expressing the nature of man, that is, the ideal of man as a rational creature, and of positive law as an ideal system expressing the nature of a unified state. For the moment these ideas were put at the service of a growing royal authority and bore fruit in the Byzantine theory of sovereignty which became classical in public law. In private law they soon took quite another turn. For a new period of growth, demanded by the expansion of society and the breaking over the bonds of authority, was at hand to make new and wholly different demands upon philosophy.

Glossators and commentators had made or shaped the law out of Roman materials for a static, locally self-sufficient, other-worldly society revering authority because authority had saved it from what it feared, regarding chiefly the security of social institutions and negligent of the individual life because in its polity the individual lived his highest life in the life of another whose greatness was the greatness of those who served him. In the seventeenth and eighteenth centuries jurists were required to make or shape a law out of these medievalized Roman materials to satisfy the wants of an active and shifting, locally interdependent, this-worldly society, impatient of authority because authority stood in the way of what it desired, and jealously individualist, since it took free individual self-assertion to be the highest good. In England the strict law made for feudal England out of Germanic materials, sometimes superficially Romanized, was likewise to be made over to do the work of administering justice to a new world. A period of legal development resulted which is strikingly analogous to the classical period of Roman law. Once more philosophy took the helm. Once more there was an infusion into law of ideas from without the law. Once more law and morals were identified in juristic thinking. Once more men held as a living tenet that all positive law was declaratory of natural law and got its real authority from the rules of natural law which it declared. Once more juridical idealism led the jurist to survey every corner of the actual law, measuring its rules by reason and shaping, extending, restricting, or building anew in order that the actual legal edifice might be a faithful copy of the ideal.

But the theory of natural law, devised for a society organized on the basis of kinship and developed for a society organized on the basis of relations, did not suffice for a society which conceived of itself as an aggregate of individuals and was reorganizing on the basis of competitive self-assertion. Again the convenient ambiguity of *ius*, which could mean not only right and law but "a right," was pressed into service and *ius naturale* gave us natural rights. The ultimate thing was not natural law as before, not merely principles of eternal validity, but natural rights, certain qualities inherent in

man and demonstrated by reason, which natural law exists
to secure and to which positive law ought to give effect. Later
these natural rights came to be the bane of juristic thinking.
Yet they achieved great things in their day. Under the influence of this theory jurists worked out a scheme of "legal
rights" that effectively secures almost the whole field of individual interests of personality and individual interests of
substance. It put a scientific foundation under the medieval
scheme of the claims and duties involved in the relation of
king to tenants in chief, out of which the judges had developed the immemorial rights of Englishmen, and enabled the
common-law rights of Englishmen to become the natural
rights of man, intrenched as such in our bills of rights. Thus
it served as a needed check upon the exuberance of growth
stimulated by the theory of natural law. It kept a certain
needed rigidity in a time when law threatened to become
wholly fluid. And this steadying influence was strengthened
from another quarter. The Roman jurisconsult was teacher,
philosopher, and practitioner in one. As a lawyer he had the
exigencies of the general security ever before him in that he
felt the imperative need of being able to advise with assurance
what tribunals would do on a given state of facts. The seven-
teenth- and eighteenth-century jurists were chiefly teachers
and philosophers. Happily they had been trained to accept
the Roman law as something of paramount authority and so
were able to give natural law a content by assuming its
identity with an ideal form of the law which they knew and
in which they had been trained. As the Roman jurisconsult
built in the image of the old law of the city, they built on
idealized Roman lines. If Roman law could no longer claim
to be embodied authority they assumed that, corrected in its
details by a juristic-philosophical critique, it was embodied
reason.

Both of these ideas, natural rights and an ideal form of the actual law of the time and place as the jural order of nature. were handed down to and put to new uses in the nineteenth century. In the growing law of the seventeenth and eighteenth centuries they were but guides to lead growth into definite channels and insure continuity and permanence in the development of rules and doctrines. Whether natural rights were conceived as qualities of the natural man or as deductions from a compact which expressed the nature of man, the point was, not that the jurist should keep his hands off lest by devising some new precept or in reshaping some old doctrine he infringe a fundamental right, but that he should use his hand freely and skillfully to shape rules and doctrines and institutions that they might be instruments of achieving the ideal of human existence in a "state of nature." For the state of nature, let us remember, was a state which expressed the ideal of man as a rational creature. If a reaction from the formal overrefinement of the eighteenth century came to identify this with a primitive simplicity, in juristic hands it was the simplicity of a rational ideal in place of the cumbrous complexity of legal systems which had become fixed in their ideas in the stage of the strict law. Thus Pothier, discussing the Roman categories of contract and rejecting them for the "natural" principle that man, as a moral creature, should keep his engagements, declares that the complex and arbitrary system of Roman law, made up of successive additions at different times to a narrow primitive stock of legally enforceable promises, is not adhered to because it is "remote from simplicity." Again the ideal form of the actual law, which gave content to natural law, was not an ideal form of historically found principles, constraining development for all time within historically fixed bounds, as in the nineteenth century, but an ideal form of the *ratio legis* —of the reason behind the rule or doctrine or institution whereby it expressed the nature of the rational human being guided only by reason and conscience in his relations with similar beings similarly guided. Attempts to fix the immutable part of law, to lay out legal charts for all time, belong to the transition to the maturity of law. The eighteenth-century projects for codification and the era of codification on the Continent, in which the results of two centuries of growth were put in systematic form to serve as the basis of a juristic new start, in form rested upon the theory of natural law. By a sheer effort of reason the jurist could work out a complete system of deductions from the nature of man and formulate them in a perfect code. Go to, let him do so! This was not the mode of thought of a period of growth but rather of one when growth had been achieved and the philosophical theory of a law of nature was called upon for a new kind of service.

At the end of the eighteenth century Lord Kenyon had determined that "Mansfield's innovations" were not to go on. Indeed some of them were to be undone. Equity was soon to be systematized by Lord Eldon and to become "almost as fixed and settled" as the law itself. The absorption of the law merchant was complete in its main lines although in details it went on for two decades. Moreover the legislative reform movement which followed only carried into detail the ideas which had come into the law in the two preceding centuries. For a time the law was assimilating what had been taken up during the period of growth and the task of the jurist was one of ordering, harmonizing, and systematizing rather than of creating. Likewise law had been codifying on the Continent. Down to the end of the nineteenth century the codes, whatever their date, in reality speak from the end of the eighteenth century and with few exceptions are all but copies of the French code of 1804. Where there were no codes the hegemony of the historical school led to a movement back to the law of Justinian which would have undone much of the progress of the last centuries. The energies of jurists were turned for a time to analysis, classification, and system as their sole task. Where codes obtained, analytical development and dogmatic exposition of the text, as a complete and final statement of the law, was to occupy jurists exclusively for the next hundred years. We may well think of this time, as it thought of itself, as a period of maturity of law. The law was taken to be complete and self-sufficient, without antinomies and without gaps, wanting only arrangement, logical development of the implications of its several rules and conceptions, and systematic exposition of its several parts. Legislation might be needed on occasion in order to get rid of archaisms which had survived the purgation of the two prior centuries. For the rest, history and analysis, bringing out the idea behind the course of development of legal doctrines and unfolding their logical consequences, were all the apparatus which the jurist required. He soon affected to ignore philosophy and often relegated it to the science of legislation, where within narrow limits it might still be possible to think of creating.

Yet the nineteenth century was no more able to get on without philosophy of law than were its predecessors. In place of one universally recognized philosophical method we find four well-marked types. But they all come to the same final results, are marked by the same spirit, and put the same shackles upon juristic activity. They are all modes of rationalizing the juristic desires of the time, growing out of the pressure of the interest in the general security by way of reaction from a period of growth and in the security of acquisitions and security of transactions in a time of economic expansion and industrial enterprise.

In the United States, since the natural law of the eighteenth-century publicists had become classical, we relied largely upon an American variant of natural law. It was not that natural law expressed the nature of man. Rather it expressed the nature of government. One form of this variant was due to our doctrine that the common law of England was in force only so far as applicable to our conditions and our institutions. The attempt to put this doctrine philosophically regards an ideal form of the received common law as natural law and takes natural law to be a body of deductions from or implications of American institutions or the nature of our polity. Within a generation the Supreme Court of one of our states laid down dogmatically that primogeniture in estates tail (which by the way is still possible in one of the oldest of the original states) could not coexist with "the axioms of the constitution" which guarantees to each state a republican form of government. More generally, however, the American variant of natural law grew out of an attempt at philosophical statement of the power of our courts with respect to unconstitutional legislation. The constitution was declaratory of principles of natural constitutional law which were to be deduced from the nature of free government. Hence constitutional questions were always only in terms questions of constitutional interpretation. They were questions of the meaning of the document, as such, only in form. In substance they were questions of a general constitutional law which transcended the text; of whether the enactment before the court conformed to principles of natural law "running back of all constitutions" and inherent in the very idea of a government of limited powers set up by a free people. Now that courts with few exceptions have given over this mode of thinking and the highest court in the land has come to apply the limitations of the fifth and fourteenth amendments as legal standards, there are some who say that we no longer have a constitutional law. For how can there be law unless a body of rules declaring a natural law which is above all human enactment? The interpretation of a written instrument, no matter by whom enacted, may be governed by law, indeed, but can yield no law. Such ideas die hard. In the language of the eighteenth century our courts sought to make our positive law, and in particular our legislation, express the nature of American political institutions; they sought so to shape it and restrain it as to make it give effect to an ideal of our polity.

Later in the nineteenth century natural law as a deduction from American institutions or from "free government" gave way to a metaphysical-historical theory worked out in continental Europe. Natural rights were deductions from a fundamental metaphysically demonstrable datum of individual free will, and natural law was an ideal critique of positive law whereby to secure these rights in their integrity. History showed us the idea of individual liberty realizing itself in legal institutions and rules and doctrines; jurisprudence developed this idea into its logical consequences and gave us a critique of law whereby we might be delivered from futile attempts to set up legal precepts beyond the necessary minimum for insuring the harmonious coexistence of the individual and his fellows. This mode of thought was well suited to a conception of law as standing between the abstract individual and society and protecting the natural rights of the former against the latter, which American law had derived from the seventeenth-century contests in England between courts and crown. It was easy to generalize this as a contest between the individual and society, and it became more easy to do so when the common-law rights of Englishmen secured by common-law courts against the crown had become the natural rights of man secured to individual men as against the state by the bills of rights.

Others in England and America turned to a utilitarian-analytical theory. The legislator was to be guided by a principle of utility. That which made for the greatest total of individual happiness was to be the lawmaker's standard. The jurist was to find universal principles by analysis of the actual law. He had nothing to do with creative activity. His work was to be that of orderly logical development of the principles reached by analysis of what he found already given in the law and improvement of the form of the law by system and logical reconciliation of details. As it was assumed that the maximum of abstract individual free self-assertion was the maximum of human happiness, in the result the legislator was to be busied with formal improvement of the law and rendering it, as Bentham put it, more "cognoscible," while the jurist was exercising a like restricted function so far as he could work with materials afforded exclusively by the law itself. Not unnaturally metaphysical and historical and analytical jurists at the end of the century were quite willing to say that their several methods were not exclusive but were complementary.

Toward the end of the last century a positivist sociological thinking tended to supersede the metaphysical historical and the utilitarian analytical. All phenomena were determined by inexorable natural laws to be discovered by observation. Moral and social and hence legal phenomena were governed by laws as completely beyond the power of conscious human control as the movements of the planets. We might discover these laws by observation of social phenomena and might learn to submit to them intelligently instead of rashly or ignorantly defying them. But we could hope to do no more. Except as he could learn to plot some part of the inevitable curve of legal development and save us from futile flyings in the face of the laws by which legal evolution was inevitably governed, the jurist was powerless. Many combined this mode of thought with or grafted it on the metaphysical-historical theory and fought valiantly against the social legislation of the last decade of the nineteenth century and the first decade of the present century with this reinforced juristic pessimism as a base. Superficially it appeared that the Greek idea of the naturally just, which in its Roman form of natural law and its eighteenth-century form of natural rights had made for a creative legal science as long as such a science had existed, had at length exhausted its possibilities.

Today, however, we hear of a revival of natural law. Philosophy of law is raising its head throughout the world. We are asked to measure rules and doctrines and institutions and to guide the application of law by reference to the end of law and to think of them in terms of social utility. We are invited to subsume questions of law and of the application of law under the social ideal of the time and place. We are called upon to formulate the jural postulates of the civilization of the time and place and to measure law and the application of law thereby in order that law may further civilization and that the legal materials handed down with the civilization of the past may be made an instrument of maintaining and furthering the civilization of the present. We are told that observation shows us social interdependence through similarity of interest and through division of labor as the central fact in human existence and are told to measure law and the application of law functionally by the extent to which they further or interfere with this interdependence. For the era of legal self-sufficiency is past. The work of assimilating what had been received into the law from without during the period of equity and natural law has been done. The possibilities of analytical and historical development of the classical materials have been substantially exhausted. While jurists have been at these tasks, a new social order has been building which makes new demands and presses upon the legal order with a multitude of unsatisfied desires. Once more we must build rather than merely improve; we must create rather than merely order and systematize and logically reconcile details. One has but to compare the law of today on such subjects as torts or public utilities or administrative law with the law of a generation ago to see that we are in a new stage of transition; to see that the juristic pessimism of the immediate past, which arose to save us from taking in more from without while what had been taken already remained undigested, will serve no longer; and to see that the jurist of tomorrow will stand in need of some new philosophical theory of law, will call for some new philosophical conception of the end of law, and at the same time will want some new steadying philosophical conception to safeguard the general security, in order to make the law which we hand down to him achieve justice in his time and place.

CHAPTER 2

The End of Law

MAKING or finding law, call it which you will, presupposes a mental picture of what one is doing and of why he is doing it. Hence the nature of law has been the chief battle-ground of jurisprudence since the Greek philosophers began to argue as to the basis of the law's authority. But the end of law has been debated more in politics than in jurisprudence. In the stage of equity and natural law the prevailing theory of the nature of law seemed to answer the question as to its end. In the maturity of law the law was thought of as something self-sufficient, to be judged by an ideal form of itself, and as something which could not be made, or, if it could be made, was to be made sparingly. The idea of natural rights seemed to explain incidentally what law was for and to show that there ought to be as little of it as possible, since it was a restraint upon liberty and even the least of such restraint demanded affirmative justification. Thus apart from mere systematic and formal improvement the theory of lawmaking in the maturity of law was negative. It told us chiefly how we should not legislate and upon what subjects we should refrain from lawmaking. Having no positive theory of creative lawmaking, the last century was little conscious of requiring or holding a theory as to the end of law. But in fact it held such a theory and held it strongly.

As ideas of what law is for are so largely implicit in ideas of what law is, a brief survey of ideas of the nature of law from this standpoint will be useful. No less than twelve conceptions of what law is may be distinguished.

First, we may put the idea of a divinely ordained rule or set of rules for human action, as for example, the Mosaic law, or Hammurapi's code, handed him ready made by the sun god, or Manu, dictated to the sages by Manu's son Bhrigu in Manu's presence and by his direction.

Second, there is an idea of law as a tradition of the old customs which have proved acceptable to the gods and hence point the way in which man may walk with safety. For primitive man, surrounded by what seem vengeful and capricious powers of nature, is in continual fear of giving offense to these powers and thus bringing down their wrath upon himself and his fellows. The general security requires that men do only those things and do them only in the way which long custom has shown at least not displeasing to the gods. Law is the traditional or recorded body of precepts in which that custom is preserved and expressed. Whenever we find a body of primitive law possessed as a class tradition by a political oligarchy it is likely to be thought of in this way, just as a body of like tradition in the custody of a priesthood is certain to be thought of as divinely revealed.

A third and closely related idea conceives of law as the recorded wisdom of the wise men of old who had learned the safe course or the divinely approved course for human conduct. When a traditional custom of decision and custom of action has been reduced to writing in a primitive code it is likely to be thought of in this way, and Demosthenes in the fourth century B.C. could describe the law of Athens in these terms.

Fourth, law may be conceived as a philosophically discovered system of principles which express the nature of things, to which, therefore, man ought to conform his conduct. Such was the idea of the Roman jurisconsult, grafted, it is true, on the second and third ideas and on a political theory of law as the command of the Roman people, but reconciled with them by conceiving of tradition and recorded wisdom and command of the people as mere declarations or reflections of the philosophically ascertained principles, to be measured and shaped and interpreted and eked out thereby. In the hands of philosophers the foregoing conception often takes another form so that, fifth, law is looked upon as a body of ascertainments and declarations of an eternal and immutable moral code.

Sixth, there is an idea of law as a body of agreements of men in politically organized society as to their relations with each other. This is a democratic version of the identification of law with rules of law and hence with the enactments and decrees of the city-state which is discussed in the Platonic *Minos*. Not unnaturally Demosthenes suggests it to an Athenian jury. Very likely in such a theory a philosophical idea would support the political idea and the inherent moral obligation of a promise would be invoked to show why men should keep the agreements made in their popular assemblies.

Seventh, law has been thought of as a reflection of the divine reason governing the universe; a reflection of that part which determines the "ought" addressed by that reason to human beings as moral entities, in distinction from the "must" which it addresses to the rest of creation. Such was the conception of Thomas Aquinas, which had great currency down to the seventeenth century and has had much influence ever since.

Eighth, law has been conceived as a body of commands of the sovereign authority in a politically organized society as to how men should conduct themselves therein, resting ultimately on whatever basis was held to be behind the authority of that sovereign. So thought the Roman jurists of the Republic and of the classical period with respect to positive law.

And as the emperor had the sovereignty of the Roman people
devolved upon him, the *Institutes* of Justinian could lay down
that the will of the emperor had the force of a law. Such a
mode of thought was congenial to the lawyers who were
active in support of royal authority in the centralizing French
monarchy of the sixteenth and seventeenth centuries and
through them passed into public law. It seemed to fit the
circumstances of parliamentary supremacy in England after
1688 and became the orthodox English juristic theory. Also
it could be made to fit a political theory of popular sovereignty in which the people were thought of as succeeding
to the sovereignty of parliament at the American Revolution
or of the French king at the French Revolution.

A ninth idea of law takes it to be a system of precepts discovered by human experience whereby the individual human
will may realize the most complete freedom possible consistently with the like freedom of will of others. This idea,
held in one form or another by the historical school, divided
the allegiance of jurists with the theory of law as command
of the sovereign during almost the whole of the past century.
It assumed that the human experience by which legal principles were discovered was determined in some inevitable
way. It was not a matter of conscious human endeavor. The
process was determined by the unfolding of an idea of right
and justice or an idea of liberty which was realizing itself
in human administration of justice, or by the operation of
biological or psychological laws or of race characters, whose
necessary result was the system of law of the time and people
in question.

Again, tenth, men have thought of law as a system of principles, discovered philosophically and developed in detail
by juristic writing and judicial decision, whereby the external life of man is measured by reason, or in another phase,
whereby the will of the individual in action is harmonized

with those of his fellow men. This mode of thought appeared in the nineteenth century after the natural-law theory in the form in which it had prevailed for two centuries had been abandoned and philosophy was called upon to provide a critique for systematic arrangement and development of details.

Eleventh, law has been thought of as a body or system of rules imposed on men in society by the dominant class for the time being in furtherance, conscious or unconscious, of its own interest. This economic interpretation of law takes many forms. In an idealistic form it thinks of the inevitable unfolding of an economic idea. In a mechanical sociological form it thinks of class struggle or a struggle for existence in terms of economics, and of law as the result of the operation of forces or laws involved in or determining such struggles. In a positivist-analytical form it thinks of law as the command of the sovereign, but of that command as determined in its economic content by the will of the dominant social class, determined in turn by its own interest. All of these forms belong to transition from the stability of the maturity of law to a new period of growth. When the idea of the self-sufficiency of law gives way and men seek to relate jurisprudence to the other social sciences, the relation to economics challenges attention at once. Moreover in a time of copious legislation the enacted rule is easily taken as the type of legal precept and an attempt to frame a theory of legislative lawmaking is taken to give an account of all law.

Finally, twelfth, there is an idea of law as made up of the dictates of economic or social laws with respect to the conduct of men in society, discovered by observation, expressed in precepts worked out through human experience of what would work and what not in the administration of justice. This type of theory likewise belongs to the end of the nineteenth century, when men had begun to look for physical or biological bases, discoverable by observation, in place of metaphysical bases, discoverable by philosophical reflection. Another form finds some ultimate social fact by observation and develops the logical implications of that fact much after the manner of the metaphysical jurist. This again results from the tendency in recent years to unify the social sciences and consequent attention to sociological theories.

Digression is worth while in order to note that each of the foregoing theories of law was in the first instance an attempt at a rational explanation of the law of the time and place or of some striking element therein. Thus, when the law has been growing through juristic activity, a philosophical theory of law, as declaratory of philosophically ascertainable principles, has obtained. When and where the growing point of law has been in legislation, a political theory of law as the command of the sovereign has prevailed. When the law has been assimilating the results of a prior period of growth, a historical theory of law as something found by experience, or a metaphysical theory of law as an idea of right or of liberty realizing in social and legal development, has tended to be dominant. For jurists and philosophers do not make these theories as simple matters of logic by inexorable development of philosophical fundamentals. Having something to explain or to expound, they endeavor to understand it and to state it rationally and in so doing work out a theory of what it is. The theory necessarily reflects the institution which it was devised to rationalize, even though stated universally. It is an attempt to state the law or the legal institution of the time and place in universal terms. Its real utility is likely to be in its enabling us to understand that body of law or that institution and to perceive what the men of the time were seeking to do with them or to make of them. Accordingly analysis of these theories is one way of getting at the ends for which men have been striving through the legal order.

What common elements may we find in the foregoing twelve pictures of what law is? For one thing, each shows us a picture of some ultimate basis, beyond reach of the individual human will, that stands fast in the whirl of change of which life is made up. This steadfast ultimate basis may be thought of as the divine pleasure or will or reason, revealed immediately or mediately through a divinely ordained immutable moral code. It may be put in the form of some ultimate metaphysical datum which is so given us that we may rest in it forever. It may be portrayed as certain ultimate laws which inexorably determine the phenomena of human conduct. Or it may be described in terms of some authoritative will for the time and place, to which the wills of others are subjected, that will deriving its authority ultimately and absolutely in some one of the preceding forms, so that what it does is by and large in no wise a matter of chance. This fixed and stable starting point is usually the feature upon which the chief emphasis is placed. Next we shall find in all theories of the nature of law a picture of a determinate and mechanically absolute mode of proceeding from the fixed and absolute starting point. The details may come from this starting point through divine revelation or a settled authoritative tradition or record, or an inevitable and infallible philosophical or logical method, or an authoritative political machinery, or a scientific system of observation, or historically verifiable ideas which are logically demonstrable to be implications of the fundamental metaphysically given datum. Third, we shall see in these theories a picture of a system of ordering human conduct and adjusting human relations resting upon the ultimate basis and derived therefrom by the absolute process. In other words, they all picture, not merely an ordering of human conduct and adjustment of human relations, which we have actually given, but something more which we should like to have, namely, a doing of these things in a fixed, absolutely predetermined way, excluding all merely individual feelings or desires of those by whom the ordering and adjustment are carried out. Thus in these subconscious picturings of the end of law it seems to be conceived as existing to satisfy a paramount social want of general security. Certainly the nineteenth-century jurist had this conception. But is this because the function of law is limited to satisfaction of that one want, or is it because that want has been most conspicuous among those which men have sought to satisfy through law, and because the ordering of human conduct by the force of politically organized society has been adapted chiefly to satisfying that one want in the social order of the past?

Today a newer and broader idea of security is appearing in a time when the world seems no longer to afford boundless opportunities, which men only need freedom to realize, in order to be assured of their reasonable expectations. So long as there are opportunities everywhere for freely exerting one's will in pursuit of what he takes to be the goods of existence, security is taken to mean a regime of ordered competition of free wills in which acquisitive competitive self-assertion is made to operate with the least friction and waste. But when and where such an ordered struggle for existence does not leave opportunities at hand for everyone, and where especially the conquest of physical nature has enormously increased the area of human wants and expectations without corresponding increase in the means of satisfying them, equality no longer means equality of opportunity. Security no longer means simply that men are to be secure in freely taking advantage of opportunities abounding around them. Men begin to assert claims to an equality of satisfaction of expectations which liberty in itself does not afford them. Quest of an ideal relation among men leads to thinking in terms of an achieved ideal relation rather than of means of achieving it. Instead of thinking of men as ideally free to achieve it, we begin to think of them as ideally already in that relation. Hence security is to be security from what may stand between them and that relation, and keeps many far from finding themselves in it. The ideal of a world in which all men are to find themselves secure in that sense may be called the humanitarian ideal. Such an ideal is increasingly affecting the law throughout the world.

If we turn to ideas which have obtained in conscious thinking about the end of law, we may recognize three which have held the ground successively in legal history and a fourth which is beginning to assert itself. The first and simplest idea is that law exists in order to keep the peace in a given society; to keep the peace at all events and at any price. This is the conception of what may be called the stage of primitive law. It puts satisfaction of the social want of general security, stated in its lowest terms, as the purpose of the legal order. So far as the law goes, other individual or social wants are ignored or are sacrificed to this one. Accordingly the law is made up of tariffs of exact compositions for every detailed injury instead of principles of exact reparation, of devices to induce or coerce submission of controversies to adjudication instead of sanctions, of regulation of self-help and self-redress instead of a general prohibition thereof, and of mechanical modes of trial which at any rate do not admit of argument instead of rational modes of trial involving debate and hence dispute and so tending to defeat the purpose of the legal order. In a society organized on the basis of kinship, in which the greater number of social wants were taken care of by the kin-organizations, there are two sources of friction: the clash of kin-interests, leading to controversies of one kindred with another, and the kinless man, for whom no kin-organization is responsible, who also has no kin-organization to stand behind him in asserting his claims. Peace between kindreds and peace between clansmen and the growing mass of nongentile population is the unsatisfied social want to which politically organized society must address itself. The system of organized kindreds gradually breaks down. Groups of kinsmen cease to be the fundamental social units. Kin-organization is replaced by political organization as the primary agency of social control. The legal unit comes to be the free citizen or the free man. In this transition regulation of self-redress and prevention of private war among those who have no strong clan-organizations to control them or respond for them are demanded by the general security. The means of satisfying these social wants are found in a legal order conceived solely in terms of keeping the peace.

Greek philosophers came to conceive of the general security in broader terms and to think of the end of the legal order as preservation of the social *status quo*. They came to think of maintaining the general security mediately through the security of social institutions. They thought of law as a device to keep each man in his appointed groove in society and thus prevent friction with his fellows. The virtue on which they insisted was *sophrosyne*, knowing the limits which nature fixes for human conduct and keeping within them. The vice which they denounced was *hybris*, willful boundbreaking—willful transgression of the socially appointed bounds. This mode of thinking follows the substitution of the city-state political organization of society for the kin-organization. The organized kindreds were still powerful. An aristocracy of the kin-organized and kin-conscious, on the one hand, and a mass of those who had lost or severed their ties of kinship or had come from without, on the other hand, were in continual struggle for social and political mastery. Also the politically ambitious individual and the masterful aristocrat were continually threatening the none-too-

stable political organization through which the general security got a precarious protection. The chief social want,
which no other social institution could satisfy, was the security of social institutions generally. In the form of maintenance of the social *status quo* this became the Greek and
thence the Roman and medieval conception of the end of
law.

Transition from the idea of law as a device to keep the
peace to the idea of law as a device to maintain the social
status quo may be seen in the proposition of Heraclitus, that
men should fight for their laws as for the walls of their city.
In Plato the idea of maintaining the social order through the
law is fully developed. The actual social order was by no
means what it should be. Men were to be reclassified and
everyone assigned to the class for which he was best fitted.
But when the classification and the assignment had been
made the law was to keep him there. It was not a device to set
him free that he might find his own level by free competition
with his fellows and free experiment with his natural powers.
It was a device to prevent such disturbances of the social order by holding each individual to his appointed place. As
Plato puts it, the shoemaker is to be only a shoemaker and
not a pilot also; the farmer is to be only a farmer and not a
judge as well; the soldier is to be only a soldier and not a man
of business besides; and if a universal genius who through
wisdom can be everything and do everything comes to the
ideal city-state, he is to be required to move on. Aristotle
puts the same idea in another way, asserting that justice is
a condition in which each keeps within his appointed sphere;
that we first take account of relations of inequality, treating
individuals according to their worth, and then secondarily
of relations of equality in the classes into which their worth
requires them to be assigned. When St. Paul exhorted wives
to obey their husbands, and servants to obey their masters,

and thus everyone to exert himself to do his duty in the class where the social order had put him, he expressed this Greek conception of the end of law.

Roman lawyers made the Greek philosophical conception into a juristic theory. For the famous three precepts to which the law is reduced in Justinian's *Institutes* come to this: Everyone is to live honorably; he is to "preserve moral worth in his own person" by conforming to the conventions of the social order. Everyone is to respect the personality of others; he is not to interfere with those interests and powers of action, conceded to others by the social order, which make up their legal personality. Everyone is to render to everyone else his own; he is to respect the acquired rights of others. The social system has defined certain things as belonging to each individual. Justice is defined in the *Institutes* as the set and constant purpose of giving him these things. It consists in rendering them to him and in not interfering with his having and using them within the defined limits. This is a legal development of the Greek idea of harmoniously maintaining the social *status quo*. The later eastern empire carried it to the extreme. Stability was to be secured by rigidly keeping everyone to his trade or calling and his descendants were to follow him therein. Thus the harmony of society and the social order would not be disturbed by individual ambition.

In the Middle Ages the primitive idea of law as designed only to keep the peace came back with Germanic law. But the study of Roman law presently taught the Roman version of the Greek conception, and the legal order was thought of once more as an orderly maintenance of the social *status quo*. This conception answered to the needs of medieval society, in which men had found relief from anarchy and violence in relations of service and protection and a social organization which classified men in terms of such relations and required them to be held to their functions as so determined. Where the Greeks thought of a stationary society corrected from time to time with reference to its nature or ideal, the Middle Ages thought of a stationary society resting upon authority and determined by custom or tradition. To each, law was a system of precepts existing to maintain this stationary society as it was.

In the feudal social order reciprocal duties involved in relations established by tradition and taken to rest on authority were the significant legal institutions. With the gradual disintegration of this order and the growing importance of the individual in a society engaged in discovery, colonization, and trade, to secure the claims of individuals to assert themselves freely in the new fields of human activity which were opening on every side became a more pressing social want than to maintain the social institutions by which the system of reciprocal duties was enforced and the relations involving those duties were preserved. Men did not so much desire that others perform for them the duties owing in some relation as that others keep hands off while they achieved what they might for themselves in a world that continually afforded new opportunities to the active and the daring. The demand was no longer that men be kept in their appointed grooves. Friction and waste were apprehended, not from men getting out of these grooves, but from attempts to hold them there by means devised to meet the needs of a different social order whereby they were made to chafe under arbitrary restraint and their powers were not utilized in the discovery and exploitation of the resources of nature, to which human powers were to be devoted in the succeeding centuries. Accordingly the end of law comes to be conceived as a making possible of the maximum of individual free self-assertion.

Transition to the newer way of thinking may be seen in the Spanish jurist-theologians of the sixteenth century. Their juristic theory was one of natural limits of activity in the relations of individuals with each other, that is, of limits to human action which expressed the rational ideal of man as a moral creature and were imposed upon men by reason. This theory differs significantly from the idea of antiquity, although it goes by the old name. The Greeks thought of a system of limiting men's activities in order that each might be kept in the place for which he was best fitted by nature— the place in which he might realize an ideal form of his capacities—and thus to preserve the social order as it stands or as it shall stand after a rearrangement. The sixteenth-century jurists of the Counter-Reformation held that men's activities were naturally limited, and hence that positive law might and should limit them in the interest of other men's activities, because all men have freedom of will and ability to direct themselves to conscious ends. Where Aristotle thought of inequalities arising from the different worth of individual men and their different capacities for the things which the social order called for, these jurists thought of a natural (i.e., ideal) equality, involved in the like freedom of will and the like power of conscious employment of one's faculties inherent in all men. Hence law did not exist to maintain the social *status quo* with all its arbitrary restraints on the will and on employment of individual powers; it existed rather to maintain the natural equality which often was threatened or impaired by the traditional restrictions on individual activity. Since this natural equality was conceived positively as an ideal equality in opportunity to do things, it could easily pass into a conception of free individual self-assertion as the thing sought, and of the legal order as existing to make possible the maximum thereof in a world abounding in undiscovered resources, undeveloped lands, and unharnessed natural forces. The latter idea took form in the seventeenth century and prevailed for two centuries thereafter, culminating in the juristic thought of the last century.

Law as a securing of natural equality became law as a securing of natural rights. The nature of man was expressed by certain qualities possessed by him as a moral, rational creature. The limitations on human activity, of which the Spanish jurist-theologians had written, got their warrant from the inherent moral qualities of men which made it right for them to have certain things and do certain things. These were their natural rights and the law existed simply to protect and give effect to these rights. There was to be no restraint for any other purpose. Except as they were to be compelled to respect the rights of others, which the natural man or ideal man would do without compulsion as a matter of reason, men were to be left free. In the nineteenth century this mode of thought takes a metaphysical turn. The ultimate thing for juristic purposes is the individual consciousness. The social problem is to reconcile conflicting free wills of conscious individuals independently asserting their wills in the varying activities of life. The natural equality becomes an equality in freedom of will. Kant rationalized the law in these terms as a system of principles or universal rules, to be applied to human action, whereby the free will of the actor may coexist along with the free will of everyone else. Hegel rationalized the law in these terms as a system of principles wherein and whereby the idea of liberty was realizing in human experience. Bentham rationalized it as a body of rules, laid down and enforced by the state's authority, whereby the maximum of happiness, conceived in terms of free self-assertion, was secured to each individual. Its end was to make possible the maximum of free individual action consistent with general free individual action. Spencer rationalized it as a body of rules, formulating the "government of the living by the dead," whereby men sought to promote the liberty of each limited only by the like liberty of all. In any of these ways of putting it, the end of law is to secure the greatest possible general individual self-assertion; to let men do freely everything they may consistently with a like free doing of everything they may by their fellow men. This is indeed a philosophy of law for discoverers and colonizers and pioneers and traders and entrepreneurs and captains of industry. Until the world became crowded, it served well to eliminate friction and to promote the widest discovery and utilization of the natural resources of human existence.

Looking back at the history of this conception, which has governed theories of the end of law for some two hundred and fifty years, we may note that it has been put to three uses. It has been used as a means of clearing away the restraints upon free economic activity which accumulated during the Middle Ages as incidents of the system of relational duties and as expressions of the idea of holding men to their place in a static social order. This negative side played an important part in the English legislative reform movement in the last century. The English utilitarians insisted upon removal of all restrictions upon individual free action beyond those necessary for securing like freedom on the part of others. This, they said, was the end of legislation. Again it has been used as a constructive idea, as in the seventeenth and eighteenth centuries, when a commercial law which gave effect to what men did as they willed it, which looked at intention and not at form, which interpreted the general security in terms of the security of transactions and sought to effectuate the will of individuals to bring about legal results, was developed out of Roman law and the custom of merchants through juristic theories of natural law. Finally it was used as a stabilizing idea, as in the latter part of the nineteenth century, when men proved that law was an evil, even if a necessary evil, that there should be as little law made as possible, since all law involved restraint upon free exertion of the will, and hence that jurist and legislator should be content to leave things legal as they are and allow the individual "to work out in freedom his own happiness or misery" on that basis.

When this last stage in the development of the idea of law as existing to promote or permit the maximum of free individual self-assertion had been reached, the juristic possibilities of the conception had been exhausted. There were no more continents to discover. Natural resources had been discovered and exploited and the need was for conservation of what remained available. The forces of nature had been harnessed to human use. Industrial development had reached large proportions, and organization and division of labor in our economic order had gone so far that anyone who would could no longer go forth freely and do anything which a restless imagination and daring ambition suggested to him as a means of gain. Although lawyers went on repeating the old formula, the law began to move in another direction. The freedom of the owner of property to do upon it whatever he liked, so he did not overstep his limits or endanger the public health or safety, began to be restricted. Nay, the law began to make men act affirmatively upon their property in fashions which it dictated, where the general health was endangered by nonaction. The power to make contracts began to be limited where industrial conditions made abstract freedom of contract defeat rather than advance full individual human life. The power of the owner to dispose freely of his property began to be limited in order to safeguard the security of the social institutions of marriage and the family. Freedom of appropriating *res nullius* and of using *res communes* came to be abridged in order to conserve the natural resources of society. Freedom of engaging in lawful callings came to be restricted, and an elaborate process of education and examination to be imposed upon those who would engage in them, lest there be injury to the public health, safety, or morals. A regime in which anyone might freely set up a corporation to engage in a public service, or freely compete in such service, was superseded by one of legal exemption of existing public utilities from destructive competition. In a crowded world, whose resources had been exploited, a system of promoting the maximum of individual self-assertion had come to produce more friction than it relieved and to further rather than to eliminate waste.

At the end of the last and the beginning of the present century, a new way of thinking grew up. Jurists began to think in terms of human wants or desires or expectations rather than of human wills. They began to think that what they had to do was not simply to equalize or harmonize wills, but, if not to equalize, at least to harmonize the satisfaction of wants. They began to weigh or balance and reconcile claims or wants or desires or expectations, as formerly they had balanced or reconciled wills. They began to think of the end of law, not as a maximum of self-assertion, but as a maximum satisfaction of wants. Hence for a time they thought of the problem of ethics, of jurisprudence, and of politics as chiefly one of valuing; as a problem of finding criteria of the relative value of interests. In jurisprudence and politics they saw that we must add practical problems of the possibility of making interests effective through governmental action, judicial or administrative. But the first question was one of the wants to be recognized—of the interests to be recognized and secured. Having inventoried the wants or claims or interests which are asserting and for which legal security is sought, we were to value them, select those to be recognized, determine the limits within which they were to be given effect in view of other recognized interests, and ascertain how far we might give them effect by law in view of the inherent limitations upon effective legal action. This mode of thinking may be seen, concealed under different terminologies, in more than one type of jurist in the present century.

Three elements contributed to shift the basis of theories as to the end of law from wills to wants, from a reconciling or harmonizing of wills to a reconciling or harmonizing of wants. The most important part was played by psychology which undermined the foundation of the metaphysical will philosophy of law. Through the movement for unification of the social sciences, economics also played an important part, especially indirectly through the attempts at economic interpretation of legal history, reinforcing psychology by showing the extent to which law had been shaped by the pressure of economic wants. Also the differentiation of society, involved in industrial organization, was no mean factor, when classes came to exist in which claims to a minimum human existence, under the standards of the given civilization, became more pressing than claims to self-assertion. Attention was turned from the nature of law to its purpose, and a functional attitude, a tendency to measure legal rules and doctrines and institutions by the extent to which they further or achieve the ends for which law exists, began to replace the older method of judging law by criteria drawn from itself. In this respect the thought of the present is more like that of the seventeenth and eighteenth centuries than that of the nineteenth century. French writers have described this phenomenon as a "revival of juridical idealism." But in truth the social utilitarianism of today and the natural-law philosophy of the seventeenth and eighteenth centuries have only this in common: Each has its attention fixed upon phenomena of growth; each seeks to direct and further conscious improvement of the law.

In its earlier form social-utilitarianism, in common with

all nineteenth-century philosophies of law, was too absolute. Its teleological theory was to show us what actually and necessarily took place in lawmaking rather than what we were seeking to bring about. Its service to the philosophy of law was in compelling us to give over the ambiguous term "right" and to distinguish between the claims or wants or demands, existing independently of law, the legally recognized or delimited claims or wants or demands, and the legal institutions, which broadly go by the name of legal rights, whereby the claims when recognized and delimited are secured. Also it first made clear how much the task of the lawmaker is one of compromise. To the law-of-nature school, lawmaking was but an absolute development of absolute principles. A complete logical development of the content implicit in each natural right would give a body of law adequate to every time and place. It is true an idea of compromise did lurk behind the theory of the metaphysical jurists in the nineteenth century. But they sought an absolute harmonizing rather than a working compromise for the time and place. Conflicting individual wills were to be reconciled absolutely by a formula which had ultimate and universal authority. When we think of law as existing to secure social interests, so far as they may be secured through an ordering of men and of human relations through the machinery of organized political society, it becomes apparent that we may reach a practicable system of compromises of conflicting human desires here and now, by means of a mental picture of giving effect to as much as we can, without believing that we have a perfect solution for all time and for every place. As the Neo-Kantians put it, we may formulate the social ideal of the time and place and try juristic problems thereby without believing ourselves competent to lay out a social and political and legal chart for all time. As the Neo-Hegelians put it, we may discover and formulate the jural postulates of the civilization of the time and place without assuming that those postulates are a complete and final picture of ultimate law, by which it must be measured for all time.

Social utilitarianism has stood in need of correction both from psychology and from sociology. It must be recognized that lawmaking and adjudication are not in fact determined precisely by a weighing of interest. In practice the pressure of wants, demands, desires will warp the actual compromises made by the legal system this way or that. In order to maintain the general security we endeavor in every way to minimize this warping. But one needs only to look below the surface of the law anywhere at any time to see it going on, even if covered up by mechanical devices to make the process appear an absolute one and the result a predetermined one. We may not expect that the compromises made and enforced by the legal order will always and infallibly give effect to any picture we may make of the nature or ends of the process of making and enforcing them. Yet there will be less of this subconscious warping if we have a clear picture before us of what we are seeking to do and to what end, and if we build in the image thereof so far as we consciously build and shape the law.

Difficulties arise chiefly in connection with criteria of value. If we say that interests are to be catalogued or inventoried, that they are then to be valued, that those which are found to be of requisite value are to be recognized legally and given effect within limits determined by the valuation, so far as inherent difficulties in effective legal securing of interests will permit, the question arises at once, How shall we do this work of valuing? Philosophers have devoted much ingenuity to the discovery of some method of getting at the intrinsic importance of various interests, so that an absolute formula may be reached in accordance wherewith it may be assured that the weightier interests intrinsically shall prevail.

But I am skeptical as to the possibility of an absolute judgment. We are confronted at this point by a fundamental question of social and political philosophy. I do not believe the jurist has to do more than recognize the problem and perceive that it is presented to him as one of securing all social interests so far as he may, of maintaining a balance or harmony among them that is compatible with the securing of all of them. The last century preferred the general security. The present century has shown many signs of preferring the individual moral and social life. I doubt whether such preferences can maintain themselves.

Social utilitarians would say, weigh the several interests in terms of the end of law. But have we any given to us absolutely? Is the end of law anything less than to do whatever may be achieved thereby to satisfy human desires? Are the limits any other than those imposed by the tools with which we work, whereby we may lose more than we gain, if we attempt to apply them in certain situations? If so, there is always a possibility of improved tools. The Greek philosopher who said that the only possible subjects of lawsuit were "insult, injury, and homicide" was as dogmatic as Herbert Spencer, who conceived of sanitary laws and housing laws in our large cities as quite outside the domain of the legal order. Better legal machinery extends the field of legal effectiveness as better machinery has extended the field of industrial effectiveness. I do not mean that the law should interfere as of course in every human relation and in every situation where someone chances to think a social want may be satisfied thereby. Experience has shown abundantly how futile legal machinery may be in its attempts to secure certain kinds of interests. What I do say is, that if in any field of human conduct or in any human relation the law, with such machinery as it has, may satisfy a social want without a disproportionate sacrifice of other claims, there is no eternal limitation inherent in the nature of things, there are no bounds imposed at creation to stand in the way of its doing so.

Let us apply some of the other theories which have been current recently. The Neo-Hegelians say: Try the claims in terms of civilization, in terms of the development of human powers to the most of which they are capable—the most complete human mastery of nature, both human nature and external nature. The Neo-Kantians say: Try them in terms of a community of free-willing men as the social ideal. Duguit says: Try them in terms of social interdependence and social function. Do they promote or do they impede social interdependence through similarity of interest and division of labor? In these formulas do we really get away from the problem of a balance compatible with maintaining all the interests, with responding to all the wants and claims and expectations, which are involved in civilized social existence?

For the purpose of understanding the law of today I am content with a picture of satisfying as much of the whole body of human wants as we may with the least sacrifice. I am content to think of law as a social institution to satisfy social wants—the claims and demands and expectations involved in the existence of civilized society—by giving effect to as much as we may with the least sacrifice, so far as such wants may be satisfied or such claims given effect by an ordering of human conduct through politically organized society. For present purposes I am content to see in legal history the record of a continually wider recognizing and satisfying of human wants or claims or desires through social control; a more embracing and more effective securing of social interests; a continually more complete and effective elimination of waste and precluding of friction in human enjoyment of the goods of existence—in short, a continually more efficacious social engineering.

CHAPTER 3

The Application of Law

THREE steps are involved in the adjudication of a controversy according to law: (1) Finding the law, ascertaining which of the many rules in the legal system is to be applied, or, if none is applicable, reaching a rule for the cause (which may or may not stand as a rule for subsequent cases) on the basis of given materials in some way which the legal system points out; (2) interpreting the rule so chosen or ascertained, that is, determining its meaning as it was framed and with respect to its intended scope; (3) applying to the cause in hand the rule so found and interpreted. In the past these have been confused under the name of interpretation. It was assumed that the function of the judge consisted simply in interpreting an authoritatively given rule of wholly extra-judicial origin by an exact process of deducing its logically implied content and in mechanically applying the rule so given and interpreted. This assumption has its origin in the stage of the strict law in the attempt to escape from the over-detail on the one hand, and the vague sententiousness on the other hand, which are characteristic of primitive law. For the most part primitive law is made up of simple, precise, detailed rules for definite narrowly defined situations. It has no general principles. The first step toward a science of law is the making of distinctions between what comes within and what does not come within the legal meaning of a rule. But a body of primitive law also often contains a certain number of sententious legal proverbs, put in striking form so as to stick in the memory but vague in their content. The strict law by means of a conception of results obtained inevitably from fixed rules and undeviating remedial proceedings seeks relief from the uncertainty inherent in the finding of a larger content for overdetailed special rules through differentiation of cases and the application of legal proverbial sayings through the "equity of the tribunal." It conceives of application of law as involving nothing but a mechanical fitting of the case with the strait jacket of rule or remedy. The inevitable adjustments and extendings and limitations, which an attempt to administer justice in this way must involve, are covered up by a fiction of interpretation in order to maintain the general security.

Philosophical rationalizing of the attempt to avoid the overpersonal administration of justice incident to the partial reversion to justice without law in the stage of equity and natural law reinforced the assumption that judicial application of law was a mechanical process and was but a phase of interpretation. In the eighteenth century it was given scientific form in the theory of separation of powers. The legislative organ made laws. The executive administered them. The judiciary applied them to the decision of controversies. It was admitted in Anglo-American legal thinking that courts must interpret in order to apply. But the interpretation was taken not to be in any wise a lawmaking and the application was taken not to involve any administrative element and to be wholly mechanical. On the Continent interpretation so as to make a binding rule for future cases was deemed to belong only to the legislator. The maturity of law was not willing to admit that judge or jurist could make anything. It was not the least service of the analytical jurisprudence of the last century to show that the greater part of what goes by the name of interpretation in this way of thinking is really a lawmaking process, a supplying of new law where no rule or no sufficient rule is at hand. "The fact is," says Gray most truly, "that the difficulties of so-called interpretation arise when the legislature has had no meaning at all; when the question which is raised on the statute never occurred to it; when what the judges have to do is, not to determine what the legislature did mean on a point which was present to its mind, but to guess what it would have intended on a point not present to its mind had the point been present." The attempt to maintain the separation of powers by constitutional prohibitions has pointed to the same lesson from another side. Lawmaking, administration, and adjudication cannot be rigidly fenced off one from the other and turned over each to a separate agency as its exclusive field. There is rather a division of labor as to typical cases and a practical or historical apportionment of the rest.

Finding the law may consist merely in laying hold of a prescribed text of a code or statute. In that event the tribunal must proceed to determine the meaning of the rule and to apply it. But many cases are not so simple. More than one text is at hand which might apply; more than one rule is potentially applicable, and the parties are contending which shall be made the basis of a decision. In that event the several rules must be interpreted in order that intelligent selection may be made. Often the genuine interpretation of the existing rules shows that none is adequate to cover the case and that what is in effect, if not in theory, a new one must be supplied. Attempts to foreclose this process by minute, detailed legislation have failed signally, as, for example, in the overgrown code of civil procedure which long obtained in New York. Providing of a rule by which to decide the cause is a necessary element in the determination of a large proportion of the causes that come before our higher tribunals, and it is often because a rule must be provided that the parties are not content to abide the decision of the court of first instance.

Cases calling for genuine interpretation are relatively few and simple. Moreover genuine interpretation and lawmaking under the guise of interpretation run into one another. In other words, the judicial function and the legislative function run into one another. It is the function of the legislative organ to make laws. But from the nature of the case it cannot make laws so complete and all embracing that the judicial organ will not be obliged to exercise a certain lawmaking function also. The latter will rightly consider this a subordinate function. It will take it to be one of supplementing, developing, and shaping given materials by means of a given technique. Nonetheless it is a necessary part of judicial power. Pushed to the extreme that regards all judicial lawmaking as unconstitutional usurpation, our political theory, a philosophical classification made over by imperfect generalization from the British constitution as it was in the seventeenth century, has served merely to intrench in the professional mind the dogma of the historical school, that legislative lawmaking is a subordinate function and exists only to supplement the traditional element of the legal system here and there and to set the judicial or juristic tradition now and then in the right path as to some particular item where it has gone astray.

In Anglo-American law we do not think of analogical development of the traditional materials of the legal system as interpretation. In Roman-law countries, where the law is made up of codes supplemented and explained by the codified Roman law of Justinian and modern usage on the basis thereof, which stands as the common law, it seems clear enough that analogical application whether of a section of the code or of a text of the Roman law is essentially the same process. Both are called interpretation. As our common law is not in the form of authoritative texts, the nature of the process that goes on when a leading case is applied by analogy, or limited in its application, or distinguished, is concealed. It does not seem on the surface to be the same process as when a text of the *Digest* is so applied or limited or distinguished. Hence it has been easy for us to assume that courts did no more than genuinely interpret legislative texts and deduce the logical content of authoritatively established traditional principles. It has been easy to accept a political theory, proceeding on the dogma of separation of powers, and to lay down that courts only interpret and apply, that all making of law must come from the legislature, that courts must "take the law as they find it," as if they could always find it ready made for every case. It has been easy also to accept a juristic theory that law cannot be made; that it may only be found, and that the process of finding it is a matter purely of observation and logic, involving no creative element. If we really believed this pious fiction, it would argue little faith in the logical powers of the bench in view of the diversity of judicially asserted doctrines on the same point which so frequently exist in our case law and the widely different opinions of our best judges with respect to them. As interpretation is difficult, when it is difficult, just because the legislature had no actual intent to ascertain, so the finding of the common law on a new point is difficult because there is no rule of law to find. The judicial and the legislative functions run together also in judicial ascertainment of the common law by analogical application of decided cases.

As interpretation on the one side runs into lawmaking and so the judicial function runs into the legislative function; on the other side interpretation runs into application and so the judicial function runs into the administrative or executive. Typically judicial treatment of a controversy is a measuring of it by a rule in order to reach a universal solution for a class of causes of which the cause in hand is but an example. Typically administrative treatment of a situation is a disposition of it as a unique occurrence, an individualization whereby effect is given to its special rather than to its general features. But administration cannot ignore the universal aspects of situations without endangering the general security. Nor may judicial decision ignore their special aspects and exclude all individualization in application without sacrificing the social interest in the individual life through making justice too wooden and mechanical. The idea that there is no administrative element in the judicial decision of causes and that judicial application of law should be a purely mechanical process goes back to Aristotle's *Politics*. Writing before a strict law had developed, in what may be called the highest point of development of primitive law, when the personal character and feelings for the time being of kings or magistrates or dicasts played so large a part in the actual workings of legal justice, Aristotle sought relief through a distinction between the administrative and the judicial. He conceived that discretion was an administrative attribute. In administration regard was to be had to times and men and special circumstances. The executive was to use a wise discretion in adjusting the machinery of government to actual situations as they arose. On the other hand, he conceived that a court should have no discretion. To him the judicial office was a Procrustean one of fitting each case to the legal bed, if necessary by a surgical operation. Such a conception met the needs of the strict law. In a stage of legal maturity it was suited to the Byzantine theory of law as the will of the emperor and of the judge as the emperor's delegate to apply and give effect to that will. In the Middle Ages it had a sufficient basis in authority and in the needs of a period of strict law. Later it fitted well into the Byzantine theory of lawmaking which French publicists adopted and made current in the seventeenth and eighteenth centuries. In the United States it seemed to be required by our constitutional provisions for a separation of powers. But in practice it has broken down no less completely than the analogous idea of entire separation of the judicial from the lawmaking function.

Almost all of the problems of jurisprudence come down to a fundamental one of rule and discretion, of administration of justice by law and administration of justice by the more or less trained intuition of experienced magistrates. Controversies as to the nature of law, whether the traditional element or the imperative element of legal systems is the typical law, controversies as to the nature of lawmaking, whether the law is found by judicial empiricism or made by conscious legislation, and controversies as to the bases of law's authority, whether in reason and science on the one hand or in command and sovereign will on the other hand, get their significance from their bearing upon this question. Controversies as to the relation of law and morals, as to the distinction of law and equity, as to the province of court and jury, as to fixed rule or wide judicial power in procedure, and as to judicial sentence and administrative individualization in punitive justice are but forms of this fundamental problem. This is not the place to discuss that problem. Suffice it to say that both are necessary elements in the administration of justice, and that instead of eliminating either we must partition the field between them. But it has been assumed that one or the other must govern exclusively, and there has been a continual movement in legal history back and forth between wide discretion and strict detailed rule, between justice without law, as it were, and justice according to law. The power of the magistrate has been a liberalizing agency in periods of growth. In the stage of equity and natural law, a stage of infusion of moral ideas from without into the law, the power of the magistrate to give legal force to his purely moral ideas was a chief instrument. Today we rely largely upon administrative boards and commissions to give legal force to ideas which the law ignores. On the other hand, rule and form with no margin of application have been the main reliance of periods of stability. The strict law sought to leave nothing to the judge beyond seeing whether the letter had been complied with. The nineteenth century abhorred judicial discretion and sought to exclude the administrative element from the domain of judicial justice. Yet a certain field of justice without law always remained and by one device or another the balance of the supposedly excluded administrative element was preserved.

In the strict law individualization was to be excluded by hard and fast mechanical procedure. In practice this procedure was corrected and the balance between rule and discretion, between the legal and the administrative, was restored by fictions and by an executive dispensing power. Roman equity has its origin in the *imperium* of the *praetor*— his royal power to dispense with the strict law in particular situations. Also English equity has its origin in the royal power of discretionary application of law and dispensing with law in particular cases, misuse of which as a political institution was one of the causes of the downfall of the Stuarts. Thus we get a third agency for restoring the balance in the form of systematic interposition of praetor or chancellor on equitable grounds, leading to a system of equity. Carried too far in the stage of equity and natural law, overdevelopment of the administrative element brings about a reaction, and in the maturity of law individualization is pushed to the wall once more. Yet this elimination of the administrative takes place more in theory and in appearance than in reality. For justice comes to be administered in large measure through the application of legal standards which admit of a wide margin for the facts of particular cases, and the application of these standards is committed to laymen or to the discretion of the tribunal. Moreover a certain judicial individualization goes on. Partly this takes the form of a margin of discretionary application of equitable remedies, handed down from the stage of equity and natural law. Partly it takes the form of ascertainment of the facts with reference to the legal result desired in view of the legal rule or of choice between competing rules in effect covering the same ground, although nominally for distinct situations. In other words, a more subtle fiction does for the maturity of law what is done for the strict law by its relatively crude procedural fictions.

Of these five agencies for preserving the administrative element in judicial justice, in periods when legal theory excludes it, two call for special consideration.

It is usual to describe law as an aggregate of rules. But unless the word rule is used in so wide a sense as to be misleading, such a definition, framed with reference to codes or by jurists whose eyes were fixed upon the law of property, gives an inadequate picture of the manifold components of a modern legal system. Rules, that is, definite, detailed provisions for definite, detailed states of fact, are the main reliance of the beginnings of law. In the maturity of law they are employed chiefly in situations where there is exceptional need of certainty in order to uphold the economic order. With the advent of legal writing and juristic theory in the transition from the strict law to equity and natural law, a second element develops and becomes a controlling factor in the administration of justice. In place of detailed rules precisely determining what shall take place upon a precisely detailed state of facts, reliance is had upon general premises for judicial and juristic reasoning. These legal principles, as we call them, are made use of to supply new rules, to interpret old ones, to meet new situations, to measure the scope and application of rules and standards and to reconcile them when they conflict or overlap. Later, when juristic study seeks to put the materials of the law in order, a third element develops, which may be called legal conceptions. These are more or less exactly defined types, to which we refer cases or by which we classify them, so that when a state of facts is classified we may attribute thereto the legal consequences attaching to the type. All of these admit of mechanical or rigidly logical application. A fourth element, however, which plays a great part in the everyday administration of justice, is of quite another character.

Legal standards of conduct appear first in Roman equity. In certain cases of transactions or relations involving good faith the formula was made to read that the defendant was to be condemned to that which in good faith he ought to give or do for or render to the plaintiff. Thus the judge had a margin of discretion to determine what good faith called for, and in Cicero's time the greatest lawyer of the day thought these *actiones bonae fidei* required a strong judge because of the dangerous power which they allowed him. From this procedural device, Roman lawyers worked out certain standards or measures of conduct, such as what an upright and diligent head of a family would do, or the way in which a prudent and diligent husbandman would use his land. In similar fashion English equity worked out a standard of fair conduct on the part of a fiduciary. Later the Anglo-American law of torts worked out, as a measure for those who are pursuing some affirmative course of conduct, the standard of what a reasonable, prudent man would do under the circumstances. Also the law of public utilities worked out standards of reasonable service, reasonable facilities, reasonable incidents of the service, and the like. In all these cases the rule is that the conduct of one who acts must come up to the requirements of the standard. Yet the significant thing is not the fixed rule but the margin of discretion involved in the standard and its regard for the circumstances of the individual case. For three characteristics may be seen in legal standards: (1) They all involve a certain moral judgment upon conduct. It is to be "fair," or "conscientious," or "reasonable," or "prudent," or "diligent." (2) They do not call for exact legal knowledge exactly applied, but for common sense about common things or trained intuition about things outside of everyone's experience. (3) They are not formulated absolutely and given an exact content, either by legislation or by judicial decision, but are relative to times and places and circumstances and are to be applied with reference to the facts of the case in hand. They recognize that within the bounds fixed each case is to a certain extent unique. In the reaction from equity and natural law, and particularly in the nineteenth century, these standards were distrusted. Lord Camden's saying that the discretion of a judge was "the law of tyrants," that it was different in different men, was "casual" and dependent upon temperament, has in it the whole spirit of the maturity of law. American state courts sought to turn the principles by which the chancellors were wont to exercise their discretion into hard and fast rules of jurisdiction. They sought to reduce the standard of reasonable care to a set of hard and fast rules. If one crossed a railroad he must "stop, look, and listen." It was negligence *per se* to get on or off a moving car, to have part of the body protruding from a railroad car, and the like. Also they sought to put the duties of public utilities in the form of definite rules with a detailed, authoritatively fixed content. All these attempts to do away with the margin of application involved in legal standards broke down. The chief result was a reaction in the course of which many states turned over all questions of negligence to juries, free even from effective advice from the bench, while many other jurisdictions have been turning over subject after subject to administrative boards and commissions to be dealt with for a season without law. In any event, whether the standard of due care in an action for negligence is applying by a jury, or the standard of reasonable facilities for transportation is applying by a public service commission, the process is one of judging of the quality of a bit of conduct under its special circumstances and with reference to ideas of fairness entertained by the layman or the ideas of what is reasonable entertained by the more or less expert commissioner. Common sense, experience, and intuition are relied upon, not technical rule and scrupulously mechanical application.

We are familiar with judicial individualization in the administration of equitable remedies. Another form, namely, individualization through latitude of application under the guise of choice or ascertainment of a rule, is concealed by the fiction of the logical completeness of the legal system and the mechanical, logical infallibility of the logical process whereby the predetermined rules implicit in the given legal materials are deduced and applied. To a large and apparently growing extent the practice of our application of law has been that jurors or courts, as the case may be, take the rules of law as a general guide, determine what the equities of the cause demand, and contrive to find a verdict or render a judgment accordingly, wrenching the law no more than is necessary. Many courts have been suspected of ascertaining what the equities of a controversy require, and then raking up adjudicated cases to justify the result desired. Often formulas are conveniently elastic so that they may or may not apply. Often rules of contrary tenor overlap, leaving a convenient no-man's-land wherein cases may be decided either way according to which rule the court chooses in order to reach a result arrived at on other grounds. Occasionally a judge is found who acknowledges frankly that

he looks chiefly at the ethical situation between the parties
and does not allow the law to interfere therewith beyond
what is inevitable.

Thus we have in fact a crude equitable application, a crude
individualization, throughout the field of judicial administration of justice. It is assumed by courts more widely than
we suspect, or at least more widely than we like to acknowl-
edge. Ostensibly there is no such power. But when one looks
beneath the surface of the law reports, the process reveals itself under the name of "implication" or in the guise of two
lines of decisions of the same tribunal upon the same point
from which it may choose at will, or in the form of what
have been termed "soft spots" in the law—spots where the
lines are so drawn by the adjudicated cases that the court
may go either way as the ethical exigencies of the special
circumstances of the case in hand may require, with no apparent transgression of what purport to be hard and fast
rules. Such has been the result of attempts to exclude the
administrative element in adjudication. In theory there is no
such thing except with respect to equitable remedies, where
it exists for historical reasons. In practice there is a great deal
of it, and that in a form which is unhappily destructive of certainty and uniformity. Necessary as it is, the method by
which we attain a needed individualization is injurious to
respect for law. If the courts do not respect the law, who
will? There is no exclusive cause of the current American
attitude toward the law. But judicial evasion and warping of
the law, in order to secure in practice a freedom of judicial
action not conceded in theory, is certainly one cause. We
need a theory which recognizes the administrative element
as a legitimate part of the judicial function and insists that
individualization in the application of legal precepts is no less
important than the contents of those precepts themselves.

Three theories of application of law obtain in the legal

science of today. The theory which has the largest following among practitioners and in dogmatic exposition of the
law is analytical. It assumes a complete body of law with no
gaps and no antinomies, given authority by the state at one
stroke and so to be treated as if every item was of the same
date as every other. If the law is in the form of a code, its
adherents apply the canons of genuine interpretation and ask
what the several code provisions mean as they stand, looked
at logically rather than historically. They endeavor to find
the preappointed code pigeonhole for each concrete case,
to put the case in hand into it by a purely logical process,
and to formulate the result in a judgment. If the law is in the
form of a body of reported decisions, they assume that those
decisions may be treated as if all rendered at the same time
and as containing implicitly whatever is necessary to the
decision of future causes which they do not express. They
may define conceptions or they may declare principles. The
logically predetermined decision is contained in the conception to which the facts are referred or involved in the principle within whose scope the facts fall. A purely logical process, exactly analogous to genuine interpretation of a legislative rule, will yield the appropriate conception from given
premises or discover the appropriate principle from among
those which superficially appear to apply. Application is
merely formulation in a judgment of the result obtained by
analysis of the case and logical development of the premises
contained in the reported decisions.

Among teachers a historical theory has the larger following. If the law is in the form of a code, the code provisions
are assumed to be in the main declaratory of the law as it previously existed; the code is regarded as a continuation and
development of pre-existing law. All exposition of the code
and of any provision thereof must begin by an elaborate
inquiry into the pre-existing law and the history and devel-

opment of the competing juristic theories among which the
framers of the code had to choose. If the law is in the form
of a body of reported decisions, the later decisions are regarded as but declaring and illustrating the principles to be
found by historical study of the older ones; as developing
legal conceptions and principles to be found by historical
study of the older law. Hence all exposition must begin with
an elaborate historical inquiry in which the idea that has been
unfolding in the course of judicial decision is revealed and
the lines are disclosed along which legal development must
move. But when the content of the applicable legal precept
is discovered in these ways, the method of applying it in no
way differs from that which obtains under the analytical
theory. The process of application is assumed to be a purely
logical one. Do the facts come within or fail to come within
the legal precept? This is the sole question for the judge.
When by historical investigation he has found out what the
rule is, he has only to fit it to just and unjust alike.

Analytical and historical theories of application of law
thus seek to exclude the administrative element wholly and
their adherents resort to fictions to cover up the judicial
individualization which nonetheless obtains in practice or else
ignore it, saying that it is but a result of the imperfect constitution of tribunals or of the ignorance or sloth of those
who sit therein. The latter explanation is no more satisfying
than the fictions, and a new theory has sprung up of late
in continental Europe which may be understood best by
calling it the equitable theory, since the methods of the English chancellor had much to do with suggesting it. To the
adherents of this theory the essential thing is a reasonable
and just solution of the individual controversy. They conceive of the legal precept, whether legislative or traditional,
as a guide to the judge, leading him toward the just result.
But they insist that within wide limits he should be free to

deal with the individual case so as to meet the demands of justice between the parties and accord with the reason and moral sense of ordinary men. They insist that application of law is not a purely mechanical process. They contend that it involves not logic only but moral judgments as to particular situations and courses of conduct in view of the special circumstances which are never exactly alike. They insist that such judgments involve intuitions based upon experience and are not to be expressed in definitely formulated rules. They argue that the cause is not to be fitted to the rule but the rule to the cause.

Much that has been written by advocates of the equitable theory of application of law is extravagant. As usually happens, in reaction from theories going too far in one direction this theory has gone too far in the other. The last century would have eliminated individualization of application. Now, as in the sixteenth- and seventeenth-century reaction from the strict law, come those who would have nothing else; who would turn over the whole field of judicial justice to administrative methods. If we must choose, if judicial administration of justice must of necessity be wholly mechanical or else wholly administrative, it was a sound instinct of lawyers in the maturity of law that led them to prefer the former. Only a saint, such as Louis IX under the oak at Vincennes, may be trusted with the wide powers of a judge restrained only by a desire for just results in each case to be reached by taking the law for a general guide. And St. Louis did not have the crowded calendars that confront the modern judge. But are we required to choose? May we not learn something from the futility of all efforts to administer justice exclusively by either method? May we not find the proper field of each by examining the means through which in fact we achieve an individualization which we deny in theory, and considering the cases in which those means operate most per-sistently and the actual administration of justice most obstinately refuses to become as mechanical in practice as we expect it to be in theory?

In Anglo-American law today there are no less than seven agencies for individualizing the application of law. We achieve an individualization in practice: (1) through the discretion of courts in the application of equitable remedies; (2) through legal standards applied to conduct generally when injury results and also to certain relations and callings; (3) through the power of juries to render general verdicts; (4) through latitude of judicial application involved in finding the law; (5) through devices for adjusting penal treatment to the individual offender; (6) through informal methods of judicial administration in petty courts, and (7) through administrative tribunals. The second and fourth have been considered. Let us look for a moment at the others.

Discretion in the exercise of equitable remedies is an outgrowth of the purely personal intervention in extraordinary cases on grounds that appealed to the conscience of the chancellor in which equity jurisdiction has its origin. Something of the original flavor of equitable interposition remains in the doctrine of personal bar to relief and in the ethical quality of some of the maxims which announce policies to be pursued in the exercise of the chancellor's powers. But it was possible for the nineteenth century to reconcile what remained of the chancellor's discretion with its mode of thinking. Where the plaintiff's right was legal but the legal remedy was not adequate to secure him in what the legal right entitled him to claim, equity gave a concurrent remedy supplementing the strict law. As the remedy in equity was supplementary and concurrent, in case the chancellor in his discretion kept his hands off, as he would if he felt that he could not bring about an equitable result, the law would still operate. The plaintiff's right was in no wise at the mercy of anyone's discretion. He merely lost an extraordinary and supplementary remedy and was left to the ordinary course of the law. Such was the orthodox view of the relation of law and equity. Equity did not alter a jot or tittle of the law. It was a remedial system alongside of the law, taking the law for granted and giving legal rights greater efficacy in certain situations. But take the case of a "hard bargain," where the chancellor in his discretion may deny specific performance. In England and in several states the damages at law do not include the value of the bargain where the contract is for the sale of land. Hence unless specific performance is granted, the plaintiff's legal right is defeated. It is notorious that bargains appeal differently to different chancellors in this respect. In the hands of some the doctrine as to hard bargains has a tendency to become wooden, as it were. There is a hard and fast rule that certain bargains are "hard" and that equity will not enforce them. In states where the value of the bargain may be recovered at law, it may well be sometimes that the bargain might as well be enforced in equity, if it is not to be canceled. But the chancellor is not unlikely to wash his hands of a hard case, saying that the court of law is more callous; let that court act, although that court is the same judge with another docket before him. In other hands, the doctrine tends to become ultra-ethical and to impair the security of transactions. In other words, the margin of discretion in application of equitable remedies tends on the one hand to disappear through crystallization of the principles governing its exercise into rigid rules, or on the other hand to become overpersonal and uncertain and capricious. Yet as one reads the reports attentively he cannot doubt that in action it is an important engine of justice; that it is a needed safety valve in the working of our legal system.

At common law the chief reliance for individualizing the application of law is the power of juries to render general verdicts, the power to find the facts in such a way as to compel a different result from that which the legal rule strictly applied would require. In appearance there has been no individualization. The judgment follows necessarily and mechanically from the facts upon the record. But the facts found were found in order to reach the result and are by no means necessarily the facts of the actual case. Probably this power alone made the common law of master and servant tolerable in the last generation. Yet exercise of this power, with respect to which, as Lord Coke expressed it, "the jurors are chancellors," has made the jury an unsatisfactory tribunal in many classes of cases. It is largely responsible for the practice of repeated new trials which makes the jury a most expensive tribunal. The crude individualization achieved by juries, influenced by emotional appeals, prejudice, and the peculiar personal ideas of individual jurors, involves quite as much injustice at one extreme as mechanical application of law by judges at the other extreme. Indeed the unchecked discretion of juries, which legislation has brought about in some jurisdictions, is worse than the hobbled court and rigid mechanical application of law from which it is a reaction.

Our administration of punitive justice is full of devices for individualizing the application of criminal law. Our complicated machinery of prosecution involves a great series of mitigating agencies whereby individual offenders may be spared or dealt with leniently. Beginning at the bottom there is the discretion of the police as to who and what shall be brought to the judicial mill. Next are the wide powers of our prosecuting officers who may ignore offenses or offenders, may dismiss proceedings in their earlier stages, may present them to grand juries in such a way that no indictment results, or may enter a *nolle prosequi* after indictment. Even if the public prosecutor desires to prosecute, the grand jury may ignore the charge. If the cause comes to trial, the petit jury may exercise a dispensing power by means of a general verdict. Next comes judicial discretion as to sentence, or in some jurisdictions, assessment of punishment by the discretion of the trial jury. Upon these are superposed administrative parole or probation and executive power to pardon. The lawyer-politician who practices in the criminal courts knows well how to work upon this complicated machinery so as to enable the professional criminal to escape as well as those or even instead of those for whom these devices were intended. They have been developed to obviate the unhappy results of a theory which would have made the punishment fit the crime mechanically instead of adjusting the penal treatment to the criminal. Here, as elsewhere, the attempt to exclude the administrative element has brought about backhanded means of individualization which go beyond the needs of the situation and defeat the purposes of the law.

Even more striking is the recrudescence of personal government, by way of reaction from an extreme of government of laws and not of men, which is involved in the setting up of administrative tribunals on every hand and for every purpose. The regulation of public utilities, apportionment of the use of the water of running streams among different appropriators, workmen's compensation, the actual duration and nature of punishment for crime, admission to and practice of professions and even of trades, the power to enter or to remain in the country, banking, insurance, unfair competition and restraint of trade, the enforcement of factory laws, of pure food laws, of housing laws and of laws as to protection from fire and the relation of principal and agent, as between farmers and commission merchants, are but some of the subjects which the living law, the law in action, is leaving to executive justice in administrative tribunals. To some extent this is required by the increasing complexity of the social order and the minute division of labor which it involves. Yet this complexity and this division of labor developed for generations in which the common-law jealousy of administration was dominant. Chiefly our revival of executive justice in the present century is one of those reversions to justice without law which are perennial in legal history. As in the case of like reversions in the past it is the forerunner of growth. It is the first form of reaction from the overrigid application of law in a period of stability. A bad adjustment between law and administration and cumbrous, ineffective, and unbusinesslike legal procedure, involving waste of time and money in the mere etiquette of justice, from which we are now coming to be delivered, were doing for a time what like conditions did in English law in the middle of the sixteenth century.

If we look back at the means of individualizing the application of law which have developed in our legal system, it will be seen that almost without exception they have to do with cases involving the moral quality of individual conduct or of the conduct of enterprises, as distinguished from matters of property and of commercial law. Equity uses its powers of individualizing to the best advantage in connection with the conduct of those in whom trust and confidence has been reposed. Legal standards are used chiefly in the law of torts, in the law of public utilities, and in the law as to fiduciary relations. Jury lawlessness is an agency of justice chiefly in connection with the moral quality of conduct where the special circumstances exclude that "intelligence without passion" which, according to Aristotle, characterizes the law. It is significant that in England today the civil jury is substantially confined to cases of fraud, defamation, malicious prosecution, assault and battery, and breach of promise of marriage. Judicial individualization through choice of a rule is most noticeable in the law of torts, in the law of domestic relations, and in passing upon the conduct of enterprises.

The elaborate system of individualization in criminal procedure has to do wholly with individual human conduct. The informal methods of petty courts are meant for tribunals which pass upon conduct in the crowd and hurry of our large cities. The administrative tribunals, which are setting up on every hand, are most called for and prove most effective as means of regulating the conduct of enterprises.

A like conclusion is suggested when we look into the related controversy as to the respective provinces of common law and of legislation. Inheritance and succession, definition of interests in property and the conveyance thereof, matters of commercial law and the creation, incidents, and transfer of obligations have proved a fruitful field for legislation. In these cases the social interest in the general security is the controlling element. But where the questions are not of interests of substance but of the weighing of human conduct and passing upon its moral aspects, legislation has accomplished little. No codification of the law of torts has done more than provide a few significantly broad generalizations. On the other hand, succession to property is everywhere a matter of statute law, and commercial law is codified or codifying throughout the world. Moreover the common law insists upon its doctrine of *stare decisis* chiefly in the two cases of property and commercial law. Where legislation is effective, there also mechanical application is effective and desirable. Where legislation is ineffective, the same difficulties that prevent its satisfactory operation require us to leave a wide margin of discretion in application, as in the standard of the reasonable man in our law of negligence and the standard of the upright and diligent head of a family applied by the Roman law, and especially by the modern Roman law, to so many questions of fault, where the question is really one of good faith. All attempts to cut down this margin have proved futile. May we not conclude that in the part of the law which has to do immediately with conduct complete justice is not to be attained by the mechanical application of fixed rules? Is it not clear that in this part of the administration of justice the trained intuition and disciplined judgment of the judge must be our assurance that causes will be decided on principles of reason and not according to the chance dictates of caprice, and that a due balance will be maintained between the general security and the individual human life?

Philosophically the apportionment of the field between rule and discretion which is suggested by the use of rules and of standards respectively in modern law has its basis in the respective fields of intelligence and intuition. Bergson tells us that the former is more adapted to the inorganic, the latter more to life. Likewise rules, where we proceed mechanically, are more adapted to property and to business transactions; and standards, where we proceed upon intuitions, are more adapted to human conduct and to the conduct of enterprises. According to him, intelligence is characterized by "its power of grasping the general element in a situation and relating it to past situations," and this power involves loss of "that perfect mastery of a special situation in which instinct rules." In the law of property and in the law of commercial transactions it is precisely this general element and its relation to past situations that is decisive. The rule, mechanically applied, works by repetition and precludes individuality in results, which would threaten the security of acquisitions and the security of transactions. On the other hand, in the hand-made as distinguished from the machine-made product, the specialized skill of the workman gives us something infinitely more subtle than can be expressed in rules. In law some situations call for the product of hands, not of machines, for they involve not repetition, where the general elements are significant, but unique events, in which the special circumstances are significant. Every promissory note is like every other.

Every fee simple is like every other. Every distribution of assets repeats the conditions that have recurred since the Statute of Distributions. But no two cases of negligence have been alike or ever will be alike. Where the call is for individuality in the product of the legal mill we resort to standards. And the sacrifice of certainty in so doing is more apparent than actual. For the certainty attained by mechanical application of fixed rules to human conduct has always been illusory.

CHAPTER 4

Liability

A SYSTEMATIST who would fit the living body of the law to his logical analytical scheme must proceed after the manner of Procrustes. Indeed, this is true of all science. In life phenomena are unique. The biologist of today sometimes doubts whether there are species and disclaims higher groups as more than conveniences of study. "Dividing lines," said a great American naturalist, "do not occur in nature except as accidents." Organization and system are logical constructions of the expounder rather than in the external world expounded. They are the means whereby we make our experience of that world intelligible and available. It is with no illusion, therefore, that I am leading you to a juristic *ultima Thule* that I essay a bit of systematic legal science on a philosophical basis. Even if it never attains a final system in which the law shall stand fast forever, the continual juristic search for the more inclusive order, the continual juristic struggle for a simpler system that will better order and better reconcile the phenomena of the actual administration of justice, is no vain quest. Attempts to understand and to expound legal phenomena lead to generalizations which profoundly affect those phenomena, and criticism of those generalizations, in the light of the phenomena they seek to explain and to which they give rise, enables us to replace them or modify them or supplement them and thus to keep the law a growing instrument for achieving expanding human desires.

One of the stock questions of the science of law is the nature and system and philosophical basis of situations in which one may exact from another that he "give or do or furnish something" (to use the Roman formula) for the advantage of the former. The classical Roman lawyer, thinking in terms of natural law, spoke of a bond or relation of right and law between them whereby the one might justly and legally exact and the other was bound in justice and law to perform. In modern times, thinking, whether he knows it or not, in terms of natural rights and by derivation of legal rights, the analytical jurist speaks of rights *in personam*. The Anglo-American lawyer, thinking in terms of procedure, speaks of contracts and torts, using the former term in a wide sense. If pressed, he may refer certain enforceable claims to exact and duties of answering to the exaction to a Romanist category of quasi-contract, satisfied to say "quasi" because on analysis they do not comport with his theory of contract, and to say "contract" because procedurally they are enforced *ex contractu*. Pressed further, he may be willing to add "quasi tort" for cases of common-law liability without fault and workmen's compensation—"quasi" because there is no fault, "tort" because procedurally the liability is given effect *ex delicto*. But cases of duties enforceable either *ex contractu* or *ex delicto* at the option of the pleader and cases where the most astute pleader is hard pushed to choose have driven us to seek something better.

Obligation, the Roman term, meaning the relation of the parties to what the analytical jurists have called a right *in personam* is an exotic in our law in that sense. Moreover the relation is not the significant thing for systematic purposes, as is shown by civilian tendencies in the phrases "active obligation" and "passive obligation" to extend the term from the relation to the capacity or claim to exact and duty to answer to the exaction. The phrase "right *in personam*" and its co-phrase "right *in rem*" are so misleading in their implications, as any teacher soon learns, that we may leave them to the textbooks of analytical jurisprudence. In this chapter I shall use the simple word "liability" for the situation whereby one may exact legally and the other is legally subjected to the exaction. Using the word in that sense, I shall inquire into the philosophical basis of liability and the system of the law on that subject as related to that basis. Yellowplush said of spelling that every gentleman was entitled to his own. We have no authoritative institutional book of Anglo-American law, enacted by sovereign authority, and hence every teacher of law is entitled to his own terminology.

So far as the beginnings of law had theories, the first theory of liability was in terms of a duty to buy off the vengeance of him to whom an injury had been done whether by oneself or by something in one's power. The idea is put strikingly in the Anglo-Saxon legal proverb, "Buy spear from side or bear it," that is, buy off the feud or fight it out. One who does an injury or stands between an injured person and his vengeance, by protecting a kinsman, a child, or a domestic animal that has wrought an injury, must compound for the injury or bear the vengeance of the injured. As the social interest in peace and order—the general security in its lowest terms—comes to be secured more effectively by regulation and ultimate putting down of the feud as a remedy, payment of composition becomes a duty rather than a privilege, or in the case of injuries by persons or things in one's power a duty alternative to a duty of surrendering the offending child or animal. The next step is to measure the composition not in terms of the vengeance to be bought off but in terms of the injury. A final step is to put it in terms of reparation. These steps are taken haltingly and merge into one another, so that we may hear of a "penalty of reparation." But the result is to turn composition for vengeance into reparation for injury. Thus recovery of a sum of money by way of penalty for a delict is the historical starting point of liability.

One's neighbor whom one had injured or who had been injured by those whom one harbored was not the only personality that might desire vengeance in a primitive society. One might affront the gods, and by one's impiety in so doing might imperil the general security, since the angered gods were not unlikely to hit out indiscriminately and to cast pestilence or hurl lightning upon just and unjust alike in the community which harbored the impious wrongdoer. Hence if, in making a promise, one called the gods to witness it was needful that politically organized society, taking over a field of social control exercised by the priesthood, give a legal remedy to the promisee lest he invoke the aid of the gods and jeopardize the general security. Again in making a promise one might call the people or the neighborhood to witness and might affront them by calling them to witness in vain. Here, too, the peace was threatened and politically organized society might give a remedy to the promisee, lest he invoke the help of his fellow citizens or his neighbors. A common case might be one where a composition was promised in this way for an injury not included in the detailed tariff of compositions that is the staple of ancient "codes." Another common case was where one who held another's property for some temporary purpose promised to return it. Such a case is lending; for before the days of coined money the difference between lending a horse to go to the next town and lending ten sheep to enable the borrower to pay a composition is not perceptible. Thus another starting point of liability is recovery of a thing certain, or what was originally the same, a sum certain, promised in such wise as to endanger the general security if the promise is not carried out. In Roman law the condiction, which is the type of actions *in per-*

sonam and thus the starting point historically of rights *in personam* and of theories of obligation, was at first a recovery of a thing certain or a sum certain due upon a promise of this sort. In juristic terms the central idea of the beginnings of liability is duty to make composition for or otherwise avert wrath arising from the affronted dignity of some personality desirous of vengeance, whether an injured individual, a god, or a politically organized society. Greek law and Roman law give the name of "insult" to legally cognizable injury to personality. Insult to a neighbor by injury to him or to one of his household, insult to the gods by impious breach of the promise they had witnessed, insult to the people by wanton disregard of the undertaking solemnly made in their presence threatened the peace and order of society and called for legal remedy.

Lawyers begin to generalize and to frame conscious theories in the later part of the stage of the strict law. At first these theories are analytical rather than philosophical. The attempt is to frame general formulas by which the rigid rules of the strict law may be reconciled where they overlap or conflict or may be distinguished in their application where such overlapping or conflict threatens. By this time, the crude beginnings of liability in a duty to compound for insult or affront to man or gods or people, lest they be moved to vengeance, has developed into liability to answer for injuries caused by oneself or done by those persons or those things in one's power, and liability for certain promises made in solemn form. Thus the basis of liability has become twofold. It rests on the one hand upon duty to repair injury. It rests on the other hand upon duty to carry out formal undertakings. It is enough for this stage of legal development that all cases of liability may be referred to these two types and that useful distinctions may be reached therefrom. Consideration of why one should be held to repair injury, and why he should be held to formal undertakings, belongs to a later stage.

Juristic theory, beginning in the transition from the strict law to the stage of equity or natural law, becomes a force in the latter stage. As the relations with which the law must deal become more numerous and the situations calling for legal treatment become more complicated, it is no longer possible to have a simple, definite, detailed rule for every sort of case that can come before a tribunal, nor a fixed, absolute form for every legal transaction. Hence, under the leadership of philosophical jurists, men turn to logical development of the "nature" or ideal form of situations and to ethical ideas of what "good faith" or "good conscience" demands in particular relations or transactions. The strict law, relying on rule and form, took no account of intention as such. The words took effect quite independently of the thought behind them. But as lawyers began to reflect and to teach something more than a class or professional tradition, as they began to be influenced by philosophy to give over purely mechanical methods and to measure things by reason rather than by arbitrary will, emphasis shifted from form to substance; from the letter to the spirit and intent. The statute was thought of as but the lawmaker's formulation of a principle of natural law. It was not the *uerba* that were efficacious, as in the strict law, which had inherited the primitive faith in the power of words and thought of the legal formula as if it were a formula of incantation possessing inherent magical force. It was the *ratio iuris*, which transcended words and formulas. So also the traditional rule was not a magic formula discovered by our fathers. It was a customary expression of a principle of natural law. Likewise the formal transaction was not a bit of private magic employed to conjure up legal liability. It was the clothing in legally recognized vestments of an intention to do what reason and good faith

demand in a given situation. When form and intention con-
curred the promisor must answer for what he undertook.
When the form used did not express or went beyond the
intention or was the product of an apparent but not a real
intention, the promisee was not to be enriched unjustly at
the promisor's expense on the sole basis of the form. Moreover the duty was to be one of doing what good faith demanded, not one of doing literally and exactly what the letter
of the undertaking called for. And although there was no
express undertaking, there might be duties implied in the
relation or situation or transaction, viewed as one of good
faith, and one might be held to a standard of action because
an upright and diligent man, who was his own master, would
so act. Such is the mode of thinking in the classical period
of the Roman law and it is closely paralleled by an independent development of juristic thought in the rise of equity and
the absorption of the law merchant in our law.

It was easy to fit the two categories, delict and formal
undertaking, which had come down from the strict law, into
the new mode of thought. The typical delict required *dolus*
—intentional aggression upon the personality or the substance of another. Indeed Aquilian *culpa*, in which the fault
did not extend to intentional aggression, is a juristic equitable development. Hence when the legal was identified with
the moral, and such identification is a prime characteristic
of this stage, the significant thing in delict seemed to be
the moral duty to repair an injury caused by willful aggression. The legal precept was *alienum non laedere*. Also the
duty to perform an intentional undertaking seemed to rest
on the inherent moral quality of a promise that made it intrinsically binding on an upright man. The legal precept was
suum cuique tribuere. Thus liability seemed to flow from
intentional action—whether in the form of aggression or in

the form of agreement. The "natural" sources of liability were delict and contract. Everything else was assimilated to one or the other of them. Liability without fault was quasi-delictal. Liability imposed by good faith to prevent unjust enrichment was quasi-contractual. The central idea had become one of the demands of good faith in view of intentional action.

In the nineteenth century the conception of liability as resting on intention was put in metaphysical rather than ethical form. Law was a realization of the idea of liberty, and existed to bring about the widest possible individual liberty. Liberty was the free will in action. Hence it was the business of the legal order to give the widest effect to the declared will and to impose no duties except in order to effectuate the will or to reconcile the will of one with the will of others by a universal law. What had been a positive, creative theory of developing liability on the basis of intention became a negative, restraining, one might say pruning, theory of no liability except on the basis of intention. Liability could flow only from culpable conduct or from assumed duties. The abstract individual will was the central point in the theory of liability. If one was not actually culpable and yet established legal precepts which were not to be denied held him answerable, it was because he was "deemed" culpable, the historical legal liability being the proof of culpability. If he had not actually assumed a duty, and yet established legal precepts which were not to be denied held him to answer for it, this must be because he had assumed some relation or professed some calling in which an undertaking to that effect was "implied" or had participated in some situation in which it was "implied"—the implication being a deduction from the liability. The bases of liability were culpable conduct and legal transaction, and these came down to an ultimate basis in will. The fundamental conception in legal liability was the conception of an act—of a manifestation of the will in the external world.

Roman law and English law begin with a set of what might be called nominate delicts or nominate torts. In Roman law there were *furtum* (conversion), *rapina* (forcible conversion), and *iniuria* (willful aggression upon personality). All these involved *dolus*, i.e., intentional aggression. The *lex Aquilia* added *damnum iniuria datum* (wrongful injury to property). Later there were added what might be called the equitable delicts of *dolus* (fraud) and *metus* (duress). Here also there was willful aggression, and the delict of *dolus* gets its name from the intentional misleading that characterizes it in Roman law as it does deceit in English law. In *damnum iniuria datum*, a wider conception of fault, as distinguished from intentional aggression, grew up by juristic development, and Aquilian *culpa*, that is, a fault causing injury to property and therefore actionable on the analogy of the *lex Aquilia*, furnished the model for the modern law. All these may be fitted to the will theory and modern systematic writers regularly do so. But noxal liability for injury done by a child or slave or domestic animal did not fit it, nor did the liability of a master of a ship, an innkeeper, or a stable keeper to respond without regard to fault. Liability for injury done by child or slave or domestic animal was enforced in a noxal action on the analogy of the action which lay for the same injury if done by the defendant in person. Hence procedurally it seemed liability for a delict involving intentional aggression, and it was possible to say that there was fault in not restraining the agency that did the injury, although no fault had to be shown nor could absence of fault be shown as a defense. There was fault because there was liability, for all liability grew out of fault. Such treadings on the tail of its own argument are very common in legal reasoning. Likewise in the case of the absolute liability of the master of a ship, the innkeeper, and the stable keeper, the institutional writers could say that they were at fault in not having proper servants, although here also fault need not be established by proof nor could want of fault be made a defense. As procedurally these liabilities arose in actions on the facts of particular cases, the jurists at first lumped them with many other forms of liability, which were not in fact dependent on intention and were enforced in actions *in factum*, as obligations arising from the special facts of cases (*obligationes ex uariis causarum figuris*). Later they were called quasi-delictual obligations and they are so designated in the fourfold classification of the *Institutes*. Buckland has remarked that in almost all of the liabilities included under quasi-delict in the *Institutes* there is liability at one's peril for the act of another, especially for one's servant, as in the noxal actions, the *actio de deiectis et effusis* (for things thrown or poured from buildings upon a way) and the *actio de recepto* against an innkeeper. In other words, in these cases one was held without regard to fault for injuries incidental to the conduct of certain enterprises or callings and for failure to restrain potentially injurious agencies which one maintained.

Modern law has given up both the nominate delicts and quasi-delict, as things of any significance. The French civil code made the idea of Aquilian *culpa* into a general theory of delictal liability, saying, "Every act of man which causes damage to another obliges him through whose fault it happened to make reparation." In other words, liability is to be based on an act, and it must be a culpable act. Act, culpability, causation, damage were the elements. This simple theory of liability for culpable causation of damage was accepted universally by civilians until late in the nineteenth century and is still orthodox. Taken up by text writers on torts in the last half of that century, it had much influence in Anglo-

American law. But along with this generalization the French code preserved a liability without fault, developed out of the noxal actions, whereby parents and teachers may be held for injuries by minors under their charge, masters for injuries by their apprentices, employers for injuries by employees, and those in charge of animals for injuries by such animals. Also it provided an absolute liability for injury by a *res ruinosa*, developed out of the Roman *cautio damni infecti*. In the case of parents, teachers, and masters of apprentices there is only a presumption of fault. They may escape by showing affirmatively that they were without fault and that what happened could not have been prevented by diligence on their part. In the case of employers no excuse is admitted. The liability is absolute. In the case of animals fault of the victim, inevitable accident, and *vis maior* may be shown affirmatively by way of defense. In the case of a *res ruinosa* there is no presumption of fault. But if the structure fell or did injury because of a defect of construction or want of repair, the owner is liable absolutely and may not show that he had no notice of the defect and no reason to suspect it, or that it was not in his power to prevent the structure from falling.

Thus it will be seen that French law came very near to a logically consistent scheme of liability for fault, and civil liability for fault only, throughout the whole delictal field. Employer's liability remained absolute, and liability for animals but little short of absolute. For the rest there was in certain cases an imposition of the burden of proof that there had been no fault, leaving the ultimate liability to rest upon a presumed fault, if want of fault was not established. Nonetheless this, the most thoroughgoing attempt to make delictal liability flow exclusively from culpability—to make it a corollary of fault and of fault only—fell short of complete attainment of its aim. Recent French authors do not hesitate to say that the attempt must be given over and that a new theory of civil delictal liability must be worked out. Meanwhile the same movement away from the simple theory of delictal liability for culpable causation of damage had taken place elsewhere on the Continent. Binding had subjected the *culpa-prinzip* to thorough analysis, and following him it had come to be rejected generally by recent German and Swiss jurists.

In the common law, as has been said, we begin likewise with a set of nominate torts—assault, battery, imprisonment, trespass on lands, trespass on chattels, conversion, deceit, malicious prosecution, slander, and libel—developed procedurally through the action of trespass and the action of trespass on the case. All of these, except trespass on lands, trespass upon possession of chattels, and conversion, are cases of intentional injury. Trespass on lands, trespass on chattels, and conversion involve more than the general security and must be considered in connection with ideas of property. The social interest in security of acquisitions demands that we be able to rely on others keeping off of our lands and not molesting our chattels; that they find out for themselves and at their own risk where they are or with whose chattels they are meddling. But even here there must be an act. If there is no act, there is no liability. To these nominate torts, each with its own special rules, coming down from the strict law, we added a new ground of liability: negligence, going on a principle not of duty to answer for aggression but of duty to answer for injuries resulting from falling short of a legal standard of conduct governing affirmative courses of action. Some, indeed, sought to give us a "tort of negligence" as a nominate tort. But it was soon recognized that in negligence we have a principle of liability dependent upon a standard, not a tort to be ranged alongside of assault or imprisonment. Later, with the rise of doctrines as to injury to ad-

vantageous relations and the failure of negligence to account
for all unintended harms of which the law actually was taking note, we developed an indefinite number of innominate
torts. Today, with the obsolescence of procedural difficulties,
there is no reason why we should not generalize, as the civil
law did at the beginning of the last century; and such a generalization was attempted in the last third of the nineteenth
century. It became orthodox common law that liability was
a corollary of fault. So far as established common-law rules
imposed a liability without fault, they were said to be historical exceptions, and some of our courts, under the influence of this theory, were willing to go a long way in abrogat-
ing them. Liability, without regard to fault, for the acts of
servants and employees was reconciled with this theory by
the fiction of representation, exposed long ago by Mr. Justice
Holmes and later by Dr. Baty. Finally it came to be thought
that no liability without fault was not merely common law
but was natural law and that any legislative imposition of
such liability was arbitrary and unreasonable in itself and
hence unconstitutional. On that theory the New York Court
of Appeals held workmen's compensation unconstitutional,
and a minority of the Supreme Court of the United States as
late as 1919 announced the same proposition.

Because of its implications for constitutional law, in view
of the increasing frequency of legislation imposing responsibility at one's peril in certain enterprises, in the case of
certain dangerous agencies and in situations where it is felt
that the loss should be borne by all of us rather than by the
luckless individual who chances to be hurt, the basis of tort
liability has become a question of moment beyond the immediate law of torts. It is a practical question of the first
importance, as well as a theoretical question of interest,
whether we are to generalize our whole system of tort liability by means of one principle of liability for fault and for

fault only, as the French sought to do and as we later sought to do largely under their influence, or, on the other hand, are to admit another source of delictal liability alongside of fault, as the French law does in fact and is coming to do in theory, and as our law has always done in fact. For in our law as it stands one may perceive readily three types of delictal liability: (1) Liability for intentional harm, (2) liability for unintentional culpable harm, (3) liability in certain cases for unintended nonculpable harm. The first two comport with the doctrine of no liability without fault. The third cannot be fitted thereto. We must either brand cases of the third type as historical anomalies, of which we are gradually to rid ourselves, or else revise our notions of tort liability. Let us remember that the nineteenth century was well advanced before we understood the subject of negligence and that before we had convinced ourselves that no liability without fault was orthodox common law, the highest court of England had given absolute liability a new field by the decision in *Rylands* v. *Fletcher*. We are not questioning a long-established dogma in Anglo-American administration of justice, therefore, when we ask whether the orthodox theory of the last generation is adequate as an analytical statement of the law that is, or as a philosophical theory of the law that ought to be. My own belief is that it is neither.

Suppose that instead of beginning with the individual free will we begin with the wants or claims involved in civilized society—as it has been put, with the jural postulates of civilized society. One such postulate, I think we should agree, is that in civilized society men must be able to assume that others will do them no intended injury—that others will commit no intentional aggressions upon them. The savage must move stealthily, avoid the sky line, and go armed. The civilized man assumes that no one will attack him and so moves among his fellow men openly and unarmed, going about his business in a minute division of labor. Otherwise there could be no division of labor beyond the differentiation of men of fighting age, as we see it in a primitive society. This postulate is at the foundation of civilized society. Everywhere *dolus* is first dealt with. The system of nominate delicts or nominate torts, both in Roman law and in our law, proceeds on this postulate.

Is it not another such postulate that in civilized society men must be able to assume that their fellow men, when they are in a course of conduct will act with due care, that is, with the care which the ordinary understanding and moral sense of the community exacts, so as not to impose an unreasonable risk of injury upon them? Such a postulate is the basis of delictal *culpa*, using *culpa* in the narrower sense, and of our doctrine of negligence. In Roman law and at one time in our law attempts were made to develop this postulate contractually. If in a transaction involving good faith—that is, an informal legal transaction—one's conduct fell short of action to which the other party was justified by the understanding of upright men in expecting him to adhere, there was contractual *culpa*; there was a violation of a promise implied in the transaction and consequent liability. We borrowed something of this mode of thought from the Romans in our law of bailments, and hence think indifferently in terms of tort or contract in that connection, although historically our action for such cases is delictal. In other connections also our law for a time sought to develop this postulate contractually by means of an "implied undertaking to use skill," for which one must answer if his skill fell short of that which the legal standard of affirmative conduct called for under the circumstances. Also in the Year Books an undertaking implied in certain relations or callings to use the skill or diligence which the relation or calling demanded is often made the basis of liability. But here the basis of liability must be found in a relation. The fiction of an undertaking to use the skill or diligence involved in a relation or calling is a juristic way of saying that one who deals with another in such a relation or with another who professes such a calling is justified in assuming the skill and diligence ordinarily involved therein, so that the law holds those in the relation or engaged in the calling to that standard in order to maintain the general security. In other words another, though closely related, postulate of civilized society is involved.

It is worth a moment's digression to suggest that such things show how little the historical categories of delict and contract represent any essential or inherent need of legal thinking. Austin thought that "the distinction of obligations (or of duties corresponding to rights against persons specifically determined) into obligations which arise from contracts, obligations which arise from injuries, and obligations which arise from incidents which are neither contracts nor injuries," was a "necessary distinction," without which a "system of law evolved in a refined community" could not be conceived. This "necessary" systematic scheme, which must be "a constituent part" of any imaginable developed legal system, is but the Roman division into obligations *ex contractu*, obligations *ex delicto*, and obligations *ex uariis causarum figuris*, in which the third category is obviously a catchall. In trying to fit our law into this necessary scheme we find three types of cases must go in the third: (a) Duties or liabilities attached by law to a relation, (b) duties imposed by law to prevent unjust enrichment, (c) duties involved in an office or calling. In the third of these our Anglo-American procedure allows recovery either *ex delicto* or *ex contractu*. In the second our law sometimes goes on a property theory of constructive trust. In the first, duties are sometimes sanctioned affirmatively by conferring legal powers or negatively by legal nonrestraint of natural powers, as in the law

of domestic relations, where the wife has a power to pledge
the husband's credit for necessaries and the law does not
interfere with the parent's administering reasonable "correction" to the child. Are we to say that these dogmatic depar-
tures of our law from the Roman scheme are inconceivable
or that because of them our law is not matured or was not
"evolved in a refined community"? Or are we to say that
Austin derived his systematic ideas, not from scientific study
of English law, but from scientific study of Roman law in a
German university? Are we to say that we cannot "imagine
coherently" a system of law which enforces warranties indifferently *ex contractu* or *ex delicto* as our law does, or which
goes further and applies the contract measure of damage *ex
delicto* as does the law of Massachusetts? But enough of this.
What we have here is not any necessary distinction. It is
rather what Austin calls a "pervading notion," to be found
generally in the systematic ideas of developed legal systems
by derivation from the Roman books. Roman law may have
a contractual conception of obligation *ex delicto*—thinking
of the delict as giving rise to a debt—and the common law
a delictal conception of liability upon contract—thinking in
terms of recovery of damages for the wrong of breaking a
promise—without much difference in the ultimate results.
The fundamental things are not tort and contract but justifiable assumptions as to the mode in which one's fellow men
will act in civilized society in many different situations of
which aggression and undertaking are but two common
types.

Returning to our second postulate of due care in affirmative courses of conduct, we may note that in the society of
today it is no less fundamental than the postulate of no intentional aggression. Aggression is the chief if not the only
form of antisocial conduct in a primitive society. Indeed a
Greek writer on law and politics of the fifth century B.C.

knew of no other subject of legal precepts. But with the development of machinery and consequent increase in human powers of action, the general security comes to be threatened quite as much by the way in which one does things as by what he does. Carelessness becomes a more frequent and more serious source of danger to the general security than aggression. Hence a set of nominate delicts requiring *dolus* is supplemented by a theory of *culpa*. Hence a set of nominate torts, characterized by intentional aggression, is supplemented by liability for negligence, and the latter becomes the more important source of legal liability in practice.

Must we not recognize also a third postulate, namely, that men must be able to assume that others, who keep things or maintain conditions or employ agencies that are likely to get out of hand or escape and do damage, will restrain them or keep them within proper bounds? Just as we may not go effectively about our several businesses in a society dependent on a minute division of labor if we must constantly be on guard against the aggressions or the want of forethought of our neighbor, so our complex social order based on division of labor may not function effectively if each of us must stay his activities through fear of the breaking loose or getting out of hand of something which his neighbor harbors or maintains. There is danger to the general security not only in what men do and the way in which they do it, but also in what they fail to do in not restraining things they maintain or agencies they employ which may do injury if not kept strictly in hand. The general security is threatened by willful aggression, by affirmative action without due regard for others in the mode of conducting it, and by harboring and maintaining things and employing agencies likely to escape or to go out of bounds and do damage. Looked at in this way, the ultimate basis of delictal liability is the social interest in the general security. This interest is threatened or infringed in three ways: (1) Intentional aggression, (2) negligent action, (3) failure to restrain potentially dangerous things which one maintains or potentially dangerous agencies which one employs. Accordingly these three are the immediate bases of delictal liability.

Controversial cases of liability without fault involve the third postulate. Systematic writers have found no difficulty in reconciling the law of negligence with the will theory of liability and the doctrine of no liability without fault. Yet they must use the term fault in a strained sense in order to fit our law of negligence with its objective standard of due care, or the Roman cases of liability for *culpa* judged by the abstract standard, into any theory of moral blameworthiness. The doctrine of liability for fault and for fault only has its roots in the stage of equity and natural law, when the moral and the legal are identified, and means that one shall respond for injuries due to morally blameworthy conduct upon his part. As Ames puts it, "the unmoral standard of acting at one's peril" is replaced by the question, "Was the act blameworthy?" But is an act blameworthy because the actor has a slow reaction time or was born impulsive or is naturally timid or is easily "rattled" and hence in an emergency does not come up to the standard of what a reasonably prudent man would do in such an emergency, as applied *ex post facto* by twelve average men in the jury box? If our use of "culpable" here were not, as it were, Pickwickian, we should allow the defendant in such cases to show what sort of man nature had made him and to call for individualization with respect to his character and temperament as well as with respect to the circumstances under which he acted. As the Romanist would say, we should apply a concrete standard of *culpa*. But what the law is really regarding is not his culpable exercise of his will but the danger to the general security if he and his fellows act affirmatively without coming up to the standard imposed to maintain that security. If he acts, he must measure up to that standard at his peril of answering for injurious consequences. Whenever a case of negligence calls for sharp application of the objective standard, fault is as much a dogmatic fiction as is representation in the liability of the master for the torts of his servant. In each case the exigencies of the will theory lead us to cover up a liability irrespective of fault, imposed to maintain the general security, by a conclusive imputation of fault to one who may be morally blameless. This is no less true of cases where we speak of "negligence *per se*."

Reconciliation of common-law absolute liabilities for the getting out of hand of things likely to escape and do damage with the doctrine of no liability without fault has been sought by means of a fiction of negligence, by pronouncing them disappearing historical anomalies, by an economic interpretation that regards them as results of class interest distorting the law, and by a theory of *res ipsa loquitur*. Blackstone resorted to the first of these. "A man is answerable," he said, "for not only his own trespass but for that of his cattle also; for if by his negligent keeping they stray upon the land of another . . . this is a trespass for which the owner must answer in damages." But note that the negligence here is a dogmatic fiction. No proof of negligence is required of the plaintiff, nor may the defendant show that there was in fact no negligence. The negligence is established by the liability, not the liability by the negligence.

In the last century it was usual to refer to absolute liability for trespassing animals, for injuries by wild animals, and for injuries by domestic animals known to be vicious, as disappearing rudiments of the old liability to make composition. The common American doctrine as to cattle running at large upon uncultivated lands seemed to confirm this. Yet one need but look beneath the surface to see that the English

rule was rejected for a time in America, not because it was
in conflict with a fundamental principle of no liability without fault, but because it presupposed a settled community,
where it was contrary to the general security to turn cattle
out to graze, whereas in pioneer American communities of
the past vacant lands which were owned and those which
were not owned could not be distinguished, and the grazing
resources of the community were often its most important
resources. The common-law rule, without regard to its basis,
was for a time inapplicable to local conditions. It is significant
that as the conditions that made the rule inapplicable have
come to an end the rule has generally re-established itself.
In England it is in full vigor so that the owner of trespassing
animals is held for disease communicated by them although
he had no knowledge or reason to suppose they were diseased.
A rule that can re-establish itself and extend its scope in this
way is not moribund. It must have behind it some basis in
the securing of social interests. Nor have the attempts of
some American courts to narrow common-law liability for
injuries by known vicious animals to cases of negligent keeping made much headway. The weight of American authority
remains with the common-law rule, and in England the Court
of Appeal has carried the rule out to the extent of holding the
owner, notwithstanding that the animal was turned loose
by the wrongful act of an intermeddling third person. Nor
have the predictions that the doctrine of *Rylands* v. *Fletcher*
would disappear from the law through the courts' smother-
ing it with exceptions—predictions commonly made at the
end of the last century—been verified in the event. In 1914
the English courts refused to limit the doctrine to adjacent
freeholders and they have since extended it to new situations.
Moreover in America, where we had been told it was de-
cisively rejected, it has been applied in the past forty years
by more than one court. The leading American cases that

profess to reject the doctrine did not involve it nor did they involve the postulate of civilized society on which, as I think, it is based. Also the Court of Appeals of New York, the leading exponent of no liability without fault, had theretofore imposed a liability without regard to negligence in the case of blasting.

An ingenious explanation of the doctrine of *Rylands* v. *Fletcher* by means of the economic interpretation of legal history demands more notice. We are told that the English courts were manned by landowners or by judges drawn from the landowning class; that the doctrine of *Rylands* v. *Fletcher* is a doctrine for landowners and so was not accepted by artisans in the United States. But consider which states applied the rule and which rejected it. It was applied in Massachusetts in 1872, in Minnesota in 1872, in Ohio in 1896, in West Virginia in 1911, in Missouri in 1913, in Texas in 1916. It was rejected by New Hampshire in 1873, by New York in 1873, by New Jersey in 1876, by Pennsylvania in 1886, by California in 1895, by Kentucky in 1903, by Indiana in 1911, by Rhode Island in 1934. Is New York a community of artisans but Massachusetts a community of landowners? Did the United States begin to change from a country of artisans to one of landowners about the year 1910 so that a drift toward the doctrine began at that time after a steady rejection of it between 1873 and 1896? *Rylands* v. *Fletcher* was decided in 1867 and is connected with the movement Dicey calls collectivism, which, he says, began in 1865. It is a reaction from the notion of liability merely as a corollary of culpability. It restrains the use of land in the interest of the general security. If this view is well taken, if it was an attempt to take account of the social interest in the general security in a crowded country, this may explain the reluctance with which it was received in the United States at first, where pioneer ideas, appropriate to a less crowded agricultural country, lingered at least to the end of the nineteenth century. In the actual American decisions, some follow *Rylands* v. *Fletcher* as an authoritative statement of the common law. Other cases go rather on the principle that liability flows from culpability. Agricultural states and industrial states alike divide along these doctrinal lines. Massachusetts and Pennsylvania, both industrial states, are on opposite sides. So are Texas and Kentucky, which are agricultural states. Massachusetts and New Jersey, each with an appointive bench, are on opposite sides, and so are Ohio and New York, each with an elective bench. In truth the Massachusetts court followed authority. In New Hampshire Chief Justice Doe was not willing to go on mere authority and decided on the general principle that liability must flow from fault.

Another view is that the doctrine of *Rylands* v. *Fletcher* is a crude attempt, when negligence and the doctrine of *res ipsa loquitur* were none too well understood, to apply the principle of the latter doctrine, and that those doctrines will suffice to reach the actual result. No doubt *res ipsa loquitur* gives a possible mode of treating cases where one maintains something likely to get out of hand and do injury. For four possible solutions may be found for such cases. One is absolute liability, as in *Rylands* v. *Fletcher*. Another is to put the burden of proof of due care on the defendant, as French law does in some cases and as is done by some American decisions and some statutes in case of fires set by locomotives. A third is to apply the doctrine of *res ipsa loquitur*. A fourth would be to require the plaintiff to prove negligence, as is done by the Supreme Court of New Jersey where a known vicious animal breaks loose. That the fourth, which is the solution required by the theory of no liability without fault, has found but two courts to uphold it, and that only in the case of vicious domestic animals, is suggestive. *Res ipsa loquitur* may easily run into a dogmatic fiction, and must do so, if made to achieve the result of the doctrine of *Rylands* v. *Fletcher*, which does not permit the defendant to go forward with proof, short of *vis maior* or the unanticipated unlawful act of a third person beyond defendant's control. The vitality and persistence of the doctrine against theoretical assault for more than a generation show that it is more than a historical anomaly or a dogmatic blunder.

Another type of common-law liability without fault, the so-called liability of the carrier as an insurer and the liability of the innkeeper, is relational and depends upon a different postulate. Nineteenth-century courts in the United States endeavored to hold down the former, restricting it because of its inconsistency with the doctrine of liability as a corollary of fault. But it has proved to have abundant vitality, has been extended by legislation in some states to carriers of passengers, and has been upheld by recent legislation everywhere.

Indeed, as was pointed out above, liability under the second postulate is not of necessity liability for fault. The standard of care is objective. One may be negligent, in that he has subjected another to an unreasonable risk of injury and injury has resulted, and yet not be morally at fault. He may have done the best he could and yet not have been able to live up to the objective standard of care exacted by the law. The natural limitations of his intelligence or his congenitally slow reaction time are not to be pronounced moral faults. If it is said that his choosing to act without being able to come up to the legal standard may be regarded as a fault, what is really laid down is that so doing is a threat to the general security. But this is the real basis of the liabilities under postulate three.

Where injuries resulted without anyone's fault and by an occurrence beyond the power of anyone other than the person injured to control, both the Roman law and the common law took it for granted that each of us must bear the risks which are inevitable in human existence. An inroad upon this proposition was made in workmen's compensation when the employer was made liable for injuries in accidents in the course of employment occurring without fault of anyone. It could be said, however, that there was here an extended application of the principle of the third postulate. At least it could be said with reason that the basic purpose was the same as that behind the third postulate. By making one who conducts an enterprise liable absolutely to repair injuries received by his employees in the course of the employment, pressure is put on the employer to do diligently all that is possible to prevent accidents from occurring. Thus the ultimate purpose is to maintain the general security. As Friedmann has well put it, there is "legal responsibility to the public flowing from the control of property." But there is a tendency today to go further. With the rise of the service state, or welfare state as it likes to call itself, a movement has been developing which goes beyond the third postulate, beyond its analogy, and behind the basis for that postulate in the maintenance of the general security. It goes upon a distinct presupposition, and if it is pushed to the extent of that presupposition may require us to remake the whole theory of liability.

When I formulated the three postulates and put them as the theoretical bases of liability, a generation ago, they belonged to the type of government which maintains peace and public order and upholds the general security. In the English-speaking world until the present generation security meant security against aggression or fault or wrongdoing of others. Recently it has been coming to mean much more, but how much more it is hard to say. At any rate it is made to include security against one's own fault, improvidence or ill luck, or even defects of character. Government is at-

tempting much more than it did in the era to which my three
jural postulates belong. The service state extends liability
beyond the basis of the third postulate in the general security.
There is more than extension. A new idea of the basis of
liability comes in and new propositions are built upon it.
The humanitarian idea seems to be thought of as requiring
reparation at someone's expense of all loss to everyone, no
matter how caused. It seems to be presupposed that in civilized society everyone may expect a full economic and social
life. The state is to fulfill this expectation. So to guarantee
full economic and social life the law must be called on, as
I have been putting it, to find an involuntary Good Samaritan
to come to the assistance of every victim of loss and perhaps
even of everyone who, for any reason, cannot keep the pace
of attaining the full measure of his expectation.

Forty years ago this took the form of what was called the
insurance theory of liability. It was a humanitarian doctrine
that injuries or losses which are the common lot of mankind
should be insured against by general sharing of the burden.
It was assumed that this could be brought about by imposing liability immediately upon someone more able to bear
the burden, who could then pass it on to all of us in charges
for services rendered the public or in prices charged for
things manufactured or produced. The heavy pressure upon
the proceeds of taxation through the multiplicity of services
now performed by the state makes it impossible for the state
to assume the role of insurer and make all of us directly responsible. But we could flatter ourselves that we were sharing
the burdens of our fellow men by holding liable someone
who could bear liability for the moment and then pass it on
to us all. How far this is actually achieved needs consideration.

In one situation, in which the law has made a great advance in recent years throughout the world, there has been
a real and immediate shifting of the burden from the luck-

less victim of injury to the public. As the law was, the state could not be held for injuries to individuals through the wrongful acts of public officers. At common law only the officers themselves who wrought the injury were personally responsible. Throughout the world in the present century there has been a growing tendency to make public funds respond for injuries to individuals brought about in the operation of governmental agencies. Like the wrongdoing servant of a public utility, the wrongdoing public officer can seldom be reached to satisfy a judgment for damages because of multiplied limitations by exemptions from execution. Duguit's teaching that the state is a great public service company could be invoked here. Obviously extension to the state of liability for willful or negligent conduct of public servants in the course of their employment may be justified by the analogy of like liability of public service companies in a polity in which the state is more and more taking over the whole domain of public welfare and undertaking to render a complete public service superseding all individual initiative or private activity. But without going so far, extension of *respondeat superior* to the state may rest on the humanitarian proposition that losses incidental to service for the benefit of all of us should be borne by all of us.

It should be noted, however, that there has been no extension to the state of absolute liability for injuries without fault of anyone. The liability for injuries due to wrongful acts of servants, when imposed on the state, may be rested on the third postulate of tort liability. It has its basis in maintaining the general security by inducing a maximum of vigilance and diligence to prevent injury on the part of those who have the control of operations having potentialities of harm. Agents as well as agencies will in everyday experience get out of hand, and the general security is menaced by this tendency. It is not necessarily to be classed with social

security, state health insurance, state unemployment insurance, and old-age pensions. Although along with them it
may be put on a general humanitarian basis, they do not
involve setting up any legal liability or depend upon maintenance of the general security.

Some other extensions of liability without fault, both
statutory and judicial, are referable to a wide application
of the principle of the third postulate in maintaining the general security. Legislation imposing penalties, without requiring criminal intent, for creating danger to health or
safety, although the offender has used all due care, is of this
type. The highest degree of diligence may be assured and
thus the general security may be promoted by such statutes
as the Pure Food and Drug Acts. As to extension by judicial
action, a relatively early case was the doctrine of the family
automobile. One court put it thus: "Where a father pro-
vides his family with an automobile for their pleasure, comfort and entertainment, the dictates of natural justice should
require that the owner should be responsible for its negligent
operation, because only by doing so, as a general rule, can
substantial justice be attained." Here the court, as was usual
at the time, took the general security to be the paramount
social interest. Substantial justice meant thorough securing
of that interest. The cases put the doctrine wholly on that
basis. A cynical critic said that ownership of an automobile
indicated such affluence that a "distribution of the economic
surplus was called for." But it was in reality based on the
same regard for the social interest in the general security that
enabled liability for trespassing animals to survive the era
of dominance of the theory of liability as necessarily only
a corollary of fault. It was not unreasonable to refuse to decide the family automobile cases on principles of agency.
Nine states adopted the doctrine while fourteen, four of them
after receiving it at first, rejected it. But judicial develop-

ment of liability in such cases was arrested by legislation imposing a general liability of the owner of an automobile for negligence of others using the car with his consent.

Today there are proposals to impose civil liability without fault in many more cases, some of them going far beyond the cases spoken of. One such proposal is to abrogate judicially the requirement of establishing negligence where injury is caused to the ultimate purchaser of a manufactured article by something only possibly referable to want of care as to the condition of the article when it left the manufacturer's hands. Another is to abrogate the category of independent contractors and apply the doctrine of *respondeat superior* to injuries through their negligence as well as those due to the negligence of an agent or servant. Another is abrogation of the requirement of causation making, for example, a bus company or a company operating a heavy truck liable to dependents of a deceased who committed suicide by throwing himself under a properly operated but rapidly moving bus or truck as a means of providing for his family. Some of these proposals are put forward on the basis of maintaining the general security. Some are urged under the insurance theory. For the most part today, however, such things are urged on a general humanitarian idea. Some way must be found for relieving all distress, loss, and frustration.

As to the first of these proposals, it cannot be put better than in the words of a concurring opinion of one of the outstanding state judges of today: "I believe that the manufacturer's negligence should no longer be singled out as a basis of plaintiff's right to recover. In my opinion it should now be recognized that a manufacturer incurs an absolute liability when an article that he has placed on the market, knowing that it is to be used without inspection, proves to have a defect that causes injury to human beings." This goes beyond the purview of the postulate that one must at his peril restrain any object or activity under his control or that he carries on that has a tendency to get out of hand and do damage. Here the defendant is not maintaining anything and nothing has got out of hand. He has put something on the market intended to go through a number of hands and ultimately reach a purchaser who will use it. If in this activity he fails in any respect to exercise due care and thereby subjects others to unreasonable risk of injury, he is liable for injuries resulting from his negligence. If the injury was caused by a defect existing latent when the article was put on the market, if up to that time he had control of it, and if in ordinary experience the defect could not have existed and been undetected if he had used due care, these facts sufficiently show negligence and he should be held. But if all that is shown is that when the article got into the hands of the plaintiff it proved defective and the plaintiff was hurt, with nothing to show how or where the defect developed or to show that it must have existed when the defendant put it on the market, to render a judgment for the plaintiff we must find a new ground of liability.

In the opinion referred to the proposed liability is put on two grounds: That those who suffer injury from defective products are unprepared to meet the consequences, and that leaving the burden to rest where it falls is a needless misfortune to the person injured since "the risk of injury can be insured by the manufacturer and distributed among the public as a cost of doing business." In other words, there may be "an overwhelming misfortune" to the person injured which the law must find how to repair, and the manufacturer can and no doubt will insure against liability. Most of the recent cases have had to do with bottled carbonated soft drinks. By no means all the establishments that put such things on the market are great corporations with ample means of procuring insurance, and the argument as to passing the loss on to the public, as will appear presently, is fallacious. We may well ask whether the underlying idea is not that the manufacturer can stand the loss better than the person injured. Is this to be a universal proposition, or is it to be applied in proportion to the degree of preponderant wealth? If I am not to be my brother's keeper but am to be his insurer, should not so radical a change in the social order come through legislation rather than through judicial decision?

Workmen's compensation does not go so far as the proposition just considered. It covers only injuries and losses in the course of the employment. But it has been coming to be extended widely to injuries through fault of the employee himself, which were at first excluded. Also it has been urged that the whole subject of accidental injuries, especially injuries in the course of operation of public service agencies of transportation and traffic accidents on the highways, should be turned over to administrative boards to be dealt with on the analogy of workmen's compensation or even on a principle beyond that analogy. In a way much of this at least may be rested upon maintenance of the general security, on a theory that the absolute liability will be a spur to the highest measure of vigilance and diligence to prevent accidents. But when this is pushed beyond cases where the conditions of accidents are under the control of the person held liable, another basis has to be sought and is usually looked for in the so-called insurance theory of liability.

In the bureau organization of the service state of today the proposition as to passing liability for damages for losses incurred by no one's fault on to the public by way of employer or public utility or industrial enterprise or manufacturer or producer is fallacious. One bureau or commission fixes rates for service. Another fixes or may be fixing prices for manufactured articles or raised products. Another has a greater or less control of wages and hours. A jury or some distinct administrative agency assesses the damages or the amount of accident compensation. Each of these agencies operates independently, subject to no effective co-ordinating power. Those that control rates and prices are zealous to keep the cost to the public as low as they may. Those that control the imposition of liability are likely to be zealous to afford the maximum of relief to the injured or to their dependents. With continual pressure upon industry and enterprise to relieve the tax-paying public of the heavy burdens that our recent humanitarian programs involve, the practical result is likely to be that the burden is shifted to the most convenient victim. Such was the solution provided by section 406 of the Soviet Civil Code. "In situations where . . . the person causing the injury is not under a duty to repair, the court may nevertheless compel him to repair the injury, depending upon his property status and that of the person injured." This section seems to have proved practically unworkable and has not been put in effect. But the idea, coupled with the proposal to do away with the requirement of causation as an element of liability and the insurance theory, would rest on some such postulate of liability as this: "In civilized society men are entitled to assume that they will be secured by the state against all loss or injury, even though the result of their own fault or own improvidence, and to that end that liability to repair all loss or injury will be cast by law on someone deemed better able to bear it." This wholesale establishing of liability without fault and without regard to maintaining the general security is to be justified by a Pecksniffian belief that in doing so we are ourselves taking on the burden of repairing all loss or damage suffered by our fellow men.

No doubt to leave the luckless victim of loss and injury attributable to no one to bear the loss is not satisfying. Yet achieving of high humanitarian purposes by the easy method of using the involuntary Good Samaritan as the Greek play-wright used the god from the machine is likewise unedifying. There ought to be a better method of making the legal order effective for humanitarian ideals than that of Robin Hood or of Lord Bramwell's pickpocket who went to the charity sermon and was so moved by the preacher's eloquence that he picked the pockets of everyone in reach and put the contents in the plate.

Obviously the law has been moving toward more stress upon the social interest in the individual life, and the law of torts is subjected to strain in consequence. Much experimentation and much trial and error are inevitable. It is by no means clear that we shall we able to attain through the law what we seem to be groping for. Perhaps what is being attempted requires exceeding the limits of effective legal action. Not all of social control can be achieved through the legal order. It may be that administrative agencies may attain ideal humanitarian results better than the courts. But experience seems to show that attempts to attain them by methods outside the law will encounter the inflexible human antipathy and resistance to subjection of men's wills to the arbitrary wills of others. It may be that some part of what is sought will prove best left to nonpolitical agencies of social control. Relief from the burden of inequality of economic condition, relief from want, relief from fear, insurance against frustration where men's ambition outruns their powers are laudable humanitarian ideals. But, although many things men had long felt were impossible have come to pass in our time, one may well feel that much, at least, of the laudable humanitarian program is beyond practical attainment by law.

Two other types of liability, contractual and relational, must receive brief notice. The former has long done valiant service for the will theory. Not only liability arising from legal transactions but liability attached to an office or calling, liability attached to relations, and liability to make restitution in case of unjust enrichment have been referred to express or implied undertaking and hence to the will of the person held. But beneath the surface the so-called contract by estoppel, the cases of acceptance of a wrongly transmitted offer, the doctrine that a public utility has no general power of contract as to facilities or rates except to liquidate the terms of its relational duties in certain doubtful cases, and cases of imposition of duties on husband or wife after marriage by change of law have caused persistent and recurring difficulties and call everywhere for a revision of our ideas. Also the objective theory of contract has undermined the very citadel of the will theory. May we not refer these phenomena, not to the will of the person bound, but to another postulate of civilized society and its corollaries? May we not say that in civilized society men must be able to assume that those with whom they deal in the general intercourse of society will act in good faith? If so, four corollaries will serve as the bases of four types of liability. For it will follow that they must be able to assume (a) that their fellow men will make good reasonable expectations created by their promises or other conduct, (b) that they will carry out their undertakings according to the expectation which the moral sentiment of the community attaches thereto, (c) that they will conduct themselves with zeal and fidelity in relations, offices, and callings, and (d) that they will restore in specie or by equivalent what comes to them by mistake or unanticipated situation whereby they receive what they could not have expected reasonably to receive under such circumstances. Thus we come back to the idea of good faith, the idea of the classical Roman jurists and of the philosophical jurists of the seventeenth century, out of which the will theory was but a metaphysical development. Only we give it a basis in social philosophy where they sought a basis in theories of the nature of transactions or of the nature of man as a moral creature.

Looking back over the whole subject, shall we not explain more phenomena and explain them better by saying that the law enforces the reasonable expectations arising out of conduct, relations, and situations, instead of that it proceeds upon willed action and willed action only, enforcing the willed consequences of declared intention, enforcing reparation for willed aggression, and enforcing reparation for culpable carrying on of willed conduct? If we explain more and explain it more completely by saying that the ultimate thing in the theory of liability is justifiable reliance under the conditions of civilized society than by saying that it is free will, we shall have done all that we may hope to do by any theory.

CHAPTER 5

Property

ECONOMIC life of the individual in society, as we know it, involves four claims. One is a claim to the control of certain corporeal things, the natural media on which human existence depends. Another is a claim to freedom of industry and contract as an individual asset, apart from free exercise of one's powers as a phase of personality, since in a highly organized society the general existence may depend to a large extent upon individual labor in specialized occupations, and the power to labor freely at one's chosen occupation may be one's chief asset. Third, there is a claim to promised advantages, to promised performances of pecuniary value by others, since in a complex economic organization with minute division of labor and enterprises extending over long periods, credit more and more replaces corporeal wealth as the medium of exchange and agency of commercial activity. Fourth, there is a claim to be secured against interference by outsiders with economically advantageous relations with others, whether contractual, social, business, official, or domestic. For not only do various relations which have an economic value involve claims against the other party to the relation, which one may demand that the law secure, but they also involve claims against the world at large that these advantageous relations, which form an important part of the substance of the individual, shall not be interfered with. Legal recognition of these individual claims, legal delimitation and securing of individual interests of substance are at the foundation of our economic organization of society. In civilized society men must be able to assume that they may control, for purposes beneficial to themselves, what they have discovered and appropriated to their own use, what they have created by their own labor, and what they have acquired under the existing social and economic order. This is a jural postulate of civilized society as we know it. The law of property in the widest sense, including incorporeal property and the growing doctrines as to protection of economically advantageous relations, gives effect to the social want or demand formulated in this postulate. So also does the law of contract in an economic order based upon credit. A social interest in the security of acquisitions and a social interest in the security of transactions are the forms of the interest in the general security which give the law most to do. The general safety, peace and order and the general health are secured for the most part by police and administrative agencies. Property and contract, security of acquisitions, and security of transactions are the domain in which law is most effective and is chiefly invoked. Hence property and contract are the two subjects about which philosophy of law has had the most to say.

In the law of liability, both for injuries and for undertakings, philosophical theories have had much influence in shaping the actual law. If they have grown out of attempts to understand and explain existing legal precepts, yet they have furnished a critique by which to judge those precepts, to shape them for the future and to build new ones out of them or upon them. This is much less true of philosophical theories of property. Their role has not been critical or creative but explanatory. They have not shown how to build but have sought to satisfy men with what they had built already. Examination of these theories is an illuminating study of how philosophical theories of law grow out of the facts of time

and place as explanations thereof, and then are given universal application as necessarily explanatory or determina-
tive of social and legal phenomena for all time and in every
place. It has been said that the philosophy of law seeks the
permanent or enduring element in the law of the time and
place. It would be quite as true to say that it seeks to find
in the law of the time and place a permanent or enduring picture of universal law.

It has been said that the individual in civilized society
claims to control and to apply to his purposes what he discovers and reduces to his power, what he creates by his labor,
physical or mental, and what he acquires under the prevailing social, economic, or legal system by exchange, purchase,
gift, or succession. The first and second of these have always
been spoken of as giving a "natural" title to property. Thus
the Romans spoke of them as modes of "natural acquisition"
by occupation or by specification (making a species, i.e.,
creation). Indeed, taking possession of what one discovers is
so in accord with a fundamental human instinct that discovery and occupation have stood in the books ever since
substantially as the Romans stated them. A striking example
of the extent to which this doctrine responds to deep-seated
human tendencies is afforded by the customs as to discovery
of mineral on the public domain upon which American mining law is founded and the customs of the old whale-fishery
as to fast-fish and loose-fish which were recognized and given
effect by the courts. But there is a difficulty in the case of
creation or specification in that except where the creation is
mental only materials must be used, and the materials or tools
employed may be another's. Hence Grotius reduced creation by labor to occupation, since if one made from what he
discovered, the materials were his by occupation, and if not,
the title of others to the materials was decisive. This controversy as to the respective claims of him who creates by

labor and him who furnishes the materials goes back to the
Roman jurists of the classical period. The Proculians awarded
the thing made to the maker because as such it had not
existed previously. The Sabinians awarded it to the owner
of the materials because without materials the new thing
could not have been made. In the maturity of Roman law a
compromise was made, and various compromises have obtained ever since. In modern times, however, the claim of
him who creates has been urged by a long line of writers
beginning with Locke and culminating in the socialists. The
Romans spoke of what one acquired under the prevailing
social, economic, or legal system as held by "civil" acquisition and conceived that the principle *suum cuique tribuere*
secured the thing so acquired as being one's own.

Roman jurists recognized that certain things were not subject to acquisition in any of the foregoing ways. Under the
influence of the Stoic idea of *naturalis ratio* they conceived
that most things were destined by nature to be controlled
by man. Such control expressed their natural purpose. Some
things, however, were not destined to be controlled by individuals. Individual control would run counter to their natural purpose. Hence they could not be the subjects of private ownership. Such things were called *res extra commercium*. They might be excluded from the possibility of individual ownership in any of three ways. It might be that
from their nature they could only be used, not owned, and
from their nature they were adapted to general use. These
were *res communes*. Or it might be that they were made for
or from their nature they were adapted to public use, that
is, use for public purposes by public functionaries or by the
political community. These were *res publicae*. Again it might
be because they had been devoted to religious purposes or
consecrated by religious acts inconsistent with private ownership. Such things were *res sanctae*, *res sacrae*, and *res reli-*

giosae. In modern law, as a result of the medieval confusion
of the power of the sovereign to regulate the use of things
(*imperium*) with ownership (*dominium*) and of the idea of
the corporate personality of the state, we have made the
second category into property of public corporations. And
this has required modern systematic writers to distinguish
between those things which cannot be owned at all, such as
human beings, things which may be owned by public corporations but may not be transferred, and things which are
owned by public corporations in full dominion. We are
also tending to limit the idea of discovery and occupation
by making *res nullius* (e.g., wild game) into *res publicae* and
to justify a more stringent regulation of individual use of
res communes (e.g., of the use of running water for irriga-
tion or for power) by declaring that they are the property
of the state or are "owned by the state in trust for the people." It should be said, however, that while in form our courts
and legislatures seem thus to have reduced everything but
the air and the high seas to ownership, in fact the so-called
state ownership of *res communes* and *res nullius* is only a sort
of guardianship for social purposes. It is *imperium*, not *dominium*. The state as a corporation does not own a river as it
owns the furniture in the state house. It does not own wild
game as it owns the cash in the vaults of the treasury. What
is meant is that conservation of important social resources requires regulation of the use of *res communes* to eliminate
friction and prevent waste, and requires limitation of the
times when, places where, and persons by whom *res nullius*
may be acquired in order to prevent their extermination. Our
modern way of putting it is only an incident of the nineteenth-century dogma that everything must be owned.

It is not hard to see how the Romans came to the distinction that has obtained in the books ever since. Some things
were part of the Roman's *familia*, were used by him upon the

public domain which he occupied, or were traded by him to those with whom he had legal power of commercial intercourse. He acquired them by discovery, by capture in war, by labor in agriculture or as an artisan, by commercial transactions or by inheritance. For these things private actions lay. Other things were no part of his or of anyone's household. They were used for political or military or religious purposes or, like rivers, were put to use by everyone without being consumed thereby. As to these, the magisterial rather than the judicial power had to be invoked. They were protected or use of them was regulated and secured by interdicts. One could not acquire them so as to maintain a private action for them. Thus some things could be acquired and conveyed and some could not. In order to be valid, however, according to juristic theory the distinction must lie in the nature of things, and it was generalized accordingly.

In a time when large unoccupied areas were open to settlement and abundant natural resources were waiting to be discovered and developed, a theory of acquisition by discovery and appropriation of *res nullius*, reserving a few things as *res extra commercium*, did not involve serious difficulty. On the other hand, in a crowded world the theory of *res extra commercium* comes to seem inconsistent with private property and the theory of discovery and occupation to involve waste of social resources. As to the latter, we may compare the law of mining and of water rights on the public domain, which developed along lines of discovery and reduction to possession under the conditions of 1849 and the federal legislation of 1866 and 1872, with recent legislation proceeding on ideas of conservation of natural resources. The former requires more consideration. For the argument that excludes some things from private ownership may seem to apply more and more to land and even to movables. Thus Herbert Spencer says, in explaining *res communes*: "If one individual interferes with the relations of another to the natural media upon which the latter's life depends, he infringes the like liberties of others by which his own are measured."

But if this is true of air and of light and of running water, men will insist upon inquiring why it is not true of land, of articles of food, of tools and implements, of capital, and even, it may be, of the luxuries upon which a truly human life depends. Also if, instead of looking at property from an ideal of a maximum of individual activity, as Spencer did, one looks at it from an ideal of a maximum effectiveness of the economic order, a distinction may be drawn, as in the Soviet law, between instruments of production, which it is assumed may be used more efficiently when socialized, and consumer's goods, "articles of personal consumption and comfort," destined only to be consumed or used for the individual life, with no potentiality of producing anything. Accordingly how to give a rational account of the so-called natural right of property and how to fix the natural limits of that right became vexed questions of philosophical jurisprudence.

Antiquity was content to maintain the economic and social *status quo* or at least to idealize it and maintain it in an ideal form. The Middle Ages were content to accept *suum cuique tribuere* as conclusive. It was enough that acquisition of land and movables and private ownership of them were part of the existing social system. Upon the downfall of authority, seventeenth- and eighteenth-century jurists sought to put natural reason behind private property as behind all other institutions. When Kant had undermined this foundation the nineteenth-century philosophical jurists sought to deduce property from a fundamental metaphysical datum; the historical jurists sought to record the unfolding of the idea of private property in human experience, thus showing the universal idea; the utilitarian demonstrated private property by his fundamental test; and the positivist established its validity and necessity by observation of human institutions and their evolution. In other words, here as elsewhere, when eighteenth-century natural law broke down jurists sought to put new foundations under the old structure of natural rights, just as natural rights had been put as a new foundation to support institutions which theretofore had found a sufficient basis in authority.

Theories by which men have sought to give a rational account of private property as a social and legal institution may be arranged conveniently in six principal groups, each including many forms. These groups may be called: (1) Natural-law theories, (2) metaphysical theories, (3) historical theories, (4) positive theories, (5) psychological theories, and (6) sociological theories.

Of the natural-law theories, some proceed on a conception of principles of natural reason derived from the nature of things, some on conceptions of human nature. The former continue the ideas of the Roman lawyers. They start with a definite principle found as the explanation of a concrete case and make it a universal foundation for a general law of property. As it has been put, they find a postulate of property and derive property therefrom by deduction. Such theories usually start either from the idea of occupation or from the idea of creation through labor. Theories purporting to be based on human nature are of three forms. Some proceed on a conception of natural rights, taken to be qualities of human nature reached by reasoning as to the nature of the abstract man. Others proceed upon the basis of a social contract expressing or guaranteeing the rights derived by reason from the nature of man in the abstract. In recent thinking a third form has arisen which may be called an economic natural law. In this form of theory a general foundation for property is derived from the economic nature of man or from the nature of man as an economic entity. These are modern theories of natural law on an economic instead of an ethical basis.

Grotius and Pufendorf may be taken as types of the older natural-law theories of property. According to Grotius, all things originally were *res nullius*. But men in society came to a division of things by agreement. Things not so divided were afterward discovered by individuals and reduced to possession. Thus things came to be subjected to individual control. A complete power of disposition was deduced from this individual control, as something logically implied therein, and this power of disposition furnished the basis for acquisition from others whose titles rested directly or indirectly upon the natural foundation of the original division by agreement or of subsequent discovery and occupation. Moreover it could be argued that the control of an owner, in order to be complete, must include not only the power to give *inter vivos* but also the power to provide for devolution after death as a sort of postponed gift. Thus a complete system of natural rights of property was made to rest mediately or immediately upon a postulated original division by agreement or a subsequent discovery and occupation. This theory should be considered in the light of the facts of the subject on which Grotius wrote and of the time when he wrote. He wrote on international law in the period of expansion and colonization at the beginning of the seventeenth century. His discussion of the philosophical foundation of property was meant as a preliminary to consideration of the title of states to their territorial domain. As things were the territories of states had come down in part from the past. The titles rested on a sort of rough adjustment among the invaders of the Roman Empire. They could be idealized as the result of a division by agreement and of successions to, or acquisitions from, those who participated therein. Another part represented new "natural" titles based on discovery and occupation in the new world. Thus a Romanized, idealized scheme of the titles by which European states of the seventeenth century held their territories becomes a universal theory of property.

Pufendorf rests his whole theory upon an original pact. He argues that there was in the beginning a "negative community." That is, all things were originally *res communes*. No one owned them. They were subject to use by all. This is called a negative community to distinguish it from affirmative ownership by co-owners. He declares that men abolished the negative community by mutual agreement and thus established private ownership. Either by the terms of this pact or by a necessary implication what was not occupied then and there was subject to acquisition by discovery and occupation, and derivative acquisition of titles proceeding from the abolition of the negative community was conceived to be a further necessary implication.

In Anglo-American law, the justification of property on a natural principle of occupation of ownerless things got currency through Blackstone. As between Locke on the one side and Grotius and Pufendorf on the other, Blackstone was not willing to commit himself to the need of assuming an original pact. Apparently he held that a principle of acquisition by a temporary power of control coextensive with possession expressed the nature of man in primitive times and that afterward, with the growth of civilization, the nature of man in a civilized society was expressed by a principle of complete permanent control of what had been occupied exclusively, including as a necessary incident of such control the *ius disponendi*. Maine has pointed out that this distinction between an earlier and a later stage in the natural right of property grew out of desire to bring the theory into accord with Scriptural accounts of the Patriarchs and their relations to the land grazed by their flocks. In either event the ultimate basis is taken to be the nature of man as a rational creature, expressed in a natural principle of control of things through occupation or in an original contract providing for such ownership.

With the revival of natural law in recent years a new phase of the justification of property upon the basis of human nature has arisen. This was suggested first by economists, who deduced property from the economic nature of man as a necessity of the economic life of the individual in society. Usually it is coupled with a psychological theory on the one side and a social-utilitarian theory on the other side. In the hands of writers on philosophy of law it has often taken on a metaphysical color. From another standpoint, what are essentially natural-law theories have been advocated by socialists, either deducing a natural right of the laborer to the whole produce of his labor from a "natural" principle of creation or carrying out the idea of natural qualities of the individual human being to the point of denying all private property as a "natural" institution and deducing a general regime of *res communes* or *res publicae*.

Metaphysical theories of property are part of the general movement that replaced seventeenth- and eighteenth-century theories of natural rights, founded on the nature of the abstract man or on an assumed compact, by metaphysical theories. They begin with Kant. He first sets himself to justify the abstract idea of *a* law of property—the idea of a system of "external *meum* and *tuum*." Here, as everywhere else, he begins with the inviolability of the individual human personality. A thing is rightfully mine, he says, when I am so connected with it that anyone who uses it without my consent does me an injury. But to justify the law of property we must go beyond cases of possession where there is an actual physical relation to the object and interference therewith is an aggression upon personality. The thing can only be mine for the purposes of a legal system of *meum* and *tuum* where I will be wronged by another's use of it when it is not actually in my possession. This raises in the first instance the question, "How is a merely juridical or rational [as distinguished from a purely physical] possession possible?" He answers the question by a metaphysical version of the occupation theory of the eighteenth century. Conceding that the idea of a primitive community of things is a fiction, the idea of a logically original community of the soil and of the things upon it, he says, has objective reality and practical juridical reality. Otherwise mere objects of the exercise of the will, exempted therefrom by operation of law, would be raised to the dignity of free-willing subjects, although they have no subjective claim to be respected. Thus the first possessor founds upon a common innate right of taking possession, and to disturb him is a wrong. The first taking of possession has "a title of right" behind it in the principle of the original common claim to possession. It results that this taker obtains a control "realized by the understanding and independent of relations of space," and he or those who derive from him may possess a parcel of land although remote from it physically. Such a possession is only possible in a state of civil society. In civil society a declaration by word or act that an external thing is mine and making it an object of the exercise of my will is "a juridical act." It involves a declaration that others are under a duty of abstaining from the use of the object. It also involves an admission that I am bound in turn toward all others with respect to the objects they have made "externally theirs." For we are brought to the fundamental principle of justice that requires each to regulate his conduct by a universal rule that will give like effect to the will of others. This is guaranteed by the legal order in civil society and gives us the regime of external mine and thine. Having thus worked out a theory of *meum* and *tuum* as legal institutions, Kant turns to a theory of acquisition, distinguishing an original and primary from a derived acquisition. Nothing is originally mine without a juridical act. The elements of this legal transaction of original acquisition are three: (1) "Prehension" of an object which belongs to no one; (2) an act of the free will interdicting all others from using it as theirs; (3) appropriation as a permanent acquisition, receiving a lawmaking force from the principle of reconciling wills according to a universal law, whereby all others are obliged to respect and act in conformity to the will of the appropriator with respect to the thing appropriated. Kant then proceeds to work out a theory of derivative acquisition by transfer or alienation, by delivery or by contract, as a legal giving effect to the individual will by universal rules, not incompatible with a like efficacy in action of all other wills. This metaphysical version of the Roman theory of occupation is evidently the link between the eighteenth century and Savigny's aphorism that all property is founded in adverse possession ripened by prescription.

When Kant's theory is examined it will be found to contain both the idea of occupation and the idea of compact. Occupation has become a legal transaction involving a unilateral pact not to disturb others in respect of their occupation of other things. But the pact does not derive its efficacy from the inherent moral force of a promise as such or the nature of man as a moral creature which holds him to promises. Its efficacy is not found in qualities of promises or of men, but in a principle of reconciling wills by a universal law, since that principle requires one who declares his will as to object A to respect the declaration of his neighbor's will as to object B. On the other hand, the idea of creation is significantly absent. Writing at the end of the eighteenth century, in view of the ideas of Rousseau, who held that the man who first laid out a plot of ground and said, "This is mine," should have been lynched, and of the interferings with vested rights in Revolutionary France, Kant was not thinking how those who had not might claim a greater share in what they produced but how those who had might claim to hold what they had.

Hegel develops the metaphysical theory further by getting rid of the idea of occupation and treating property as a realization of the idea of liberty. Property, he says, "makes objective my personal, individual will." In order to reach the complete liberty involved in the idea of liberty, one must give his liberty an external sphere. Hence a person has a right to direct his will upon an external object and an object on which it is so directed becomes his. It is not an end in itself; it gets its whole rational significance from his will. Thus when one appropriates a thing, fundamentally he manifests the majesty of his will by demonstrating that external objects that have no wills are not self-sufficient and are not ends in themselves. It follows that the demand for equality in the division of the soil and in other forms of wealth is superficial. For, he argues, differences of wealth are due to accidents of external nature that give to what A has impressed with his will greater value than to what B has impressed with his, and to the infinite diversity of individual mind and character that leads A to attach his will to this and B to attach his will to that. Men are equal as persons. With respect to the principle of possession they stand alike. Everyone must have property of some sort in order to be free. Beyond this, "among persons differently endowed inequality must result and equality would be wrong."

Nineteenth-century metaphysical theories of property carry out these ideas or develop this method. And it is to be noted that they are all open to attack from the standpoint of the theory of *res extra commercium*. Thus Hegel's theory comes to this: Personality involves exercise of the will with

respect to things. When one has exercised his will with respect to a thing and so has acquired a power of control over
it, other wills are excluded from this thing and are to be directed toward objects with which other personalities have
not been so identified. So long as there are vacant lands to
occupy, undeveloped regions awaiting the pioneer, unex-
ploited natural resources awaiting the prospector—in short,
so long as there are enough physical objects in reach, if one
may so put it, to go round—this would be consistent with
the nineteenth-century theory of justice. But when, as at the
end of the nineteenth century, the world becomes crowded
and its natural resources have been appropriated and exploited, so that there is a defect in material nature whereby
such exercise of the will by some leaves no objects upon
which the wills of others may be exerted, or a deficiency
such as to prevent any substantial exertion of the will, it is
difficult to see how Hegel's argument may be reconciled
with the argument put behind the conception of *res extra
commercium.* Miller, a Scotch Hegelian, seeks to meet this
difficulty. He says that beyond what is needed for the natural
existence and development of the person, property "can only
be held as a trust for the state." In modern times, however, a
periodical redistribution, as in antiquity, is economically in-
admissible. Yet if anyone's holdings were to exceed the
bounds of reason, "the legislature would undoubtedly interfere on behalf of society and prevent the wrong which
would be done by caricaturing an abstract right." In view of
our bills of rights, an American Hegelian could not invoke
the *deus ex machina* of an act of Parliament so conveniently.
Perhaps he would fall back on graduated taxation and inheritance taxes. But does not Miller when hard pressed resort
to something very like social-utilitarianism?

Lorimer connects the metaphysical theory with theories
resting on human nature. To begin with, he deduces the

whole system of property from a fundamental proposition that "the right to be and to continue to be implies a right to the conditions of existence." Accordingly he says that the idea of property is inseparably connected "not only with the life of man but with organic existence in general"; that "life confers rights to its exercise corresponding in extent to the powers of which it consists." When, however, this is applied in explaining the basis of the present proprietary system in all its details resort must be had to a type of artificial reasoning similar to that employed by the jurists of the seventeenth and eighteenth centuries. The abstract idea of ownership is not the only thing the legal philosopher has to consider. Moreover the reasoning by which that application is made may not be reconciled with the arguments by which the doctrine of *res extra commercium* is regarded also as a bit of natural law.

Although it purports to be wholly different, the positive theory of the basis of property is essentially the same as the metaphysical. Thus Spencer's theory is a deduction from a fundamental "law of equal freedom" verified by observation of the facts of primitive society. But the "law of equal freedom" supposed to be ascertained by observation, in the same way in which physical or chemical laws are ascertained, is in fact, as has often been pointed out, Kant's formula of justice. And the verification of deductions from this law by observation of the facts of primitive civilization is not essentially different from the verification of the deductions from the metaphysical fundamental law carried on by the historical jurists. The metaphysical jurist reached a principle metaphysically and deduced property therefrom. The historical jurist thereupon verified the deduction by showing the same principle as the idea realizing itself in legal history. In the hands of the Comtian positivists the same principle is reached by observation, the same deduction is made therefrom, and the deduction is verified by finding the institution latent in primitive society and unfolding with the development of civilization. The most notable difference is that the metaphysical and historical jurists rely chiefly on primitive occupation of ownerless things, while the positivists have been inclined to lay stress upon creation of new things by labor. In any event, laying aside the verification for the moment, the deduction as made by Spencer involves the same difficulties as those involved in the metaphysical deduction. Moreover, like the metaphysical deduction, it accounts for an abstract idea of private property rather than for the regime that actually exists. Inequalities are assumed to be due to "greater strength, greater ingenuity or greater application" of those who have acquired more than their fellows. Hence, as the end of law is taken to be the bringing about of a maximum of individual free self-assertion, any interference with one's holding the fruits of his greater strength or greater ingenuity or greater application, and his resulting greater activity in creative or acquisitive self-assertion, would contravene the very purpose of the legal order. It will be noted also that this theory, like all that had gone before, assumes a complete *ius disponendi* as implied in the very notion of property. But does not this also require demonstration? Is the *ius disponendi* implied in the idea which they demonstrate, or is it only an incident of the institution they are seeking to explain by the demonstration?

Historical jurists have maintained their theory on the basis of two propositions: (1) The conception of private property, like the conception of individual personality, has had slow but steady development from the beginnings of law; (2) individual ownership has grown out of group rights just as individual interests of personality have been disentangled gradually from group interests. Let us look at each of these propositions in some detail.

If we examine the law of property analytically we may see three grades or stages in the power or capacity which men have of influencing the acts of others with respect to corporeal objects. One is a mere condition of fact, a mere physical holding of or physical control over the thing without any other element whatever. The Roman jurists called this natural possession. We call it custody. Writers on analytical jurisprudence regard it as an element of possession. But this natural possession is something that may exist independently of law or of the state, as in the so-called *pedis possessio* of American mining law, where, before law or state authority had been extended to the public domain in the mining country, the miners recognized the claim of one who was actually digging to dig without molestation at that spot. The mere having of an object in one's actual grasp gives an advantage. But it may be only an advantage depending on one's strength or on recognition of and respect for his personality by his fellow men. It is not a legal advantage except as the law protects personality. It is the physical person of the one in natural possession which is secured, not his relation to the thing held. Analytically the next grade or stage is what the Romanist calls juristic possession as distinguished from natural possession. This is a legal development of the extra-legal idea of custody. Where custody or the ability to reproduce a condition of custody is coupled with the mental element of intention to hold for one's own purposes, the legal order confers on one who so holds a capacity protected and maintained by law so to hold, and a claim to have the thing restored to his immediate physical control should he be deprived of it. As the Romanist puts it, in the case of natural possession the law secures the relation of the physical person to the object; in juristic possession the law secures the relation of the will to the object. In the highest grade of proprietary relation, ownership, the law goes much further and secures to men the exclusive or ultimate enjoyment or control of objects far beyond their capacity either to hold in custody or to possess—that is, beyond what they could hold by physical force and beyond what they could actually hold even by the help of the state. Natural possession is a conception of pure fact in no degree dependent upon law. The legally significant thing is the interest of the natural possessor in his personality. Possession or juristic possession is a conception of fact and law, existing as a pure relation of fact, independent of legal origin but protected and maintained by law without regard to interference with personality. Ownership is a purely legal conception having its origin in and depending on the law.

In general the historical development of the law of property follows the line thus indicated by analysis. In the most primitive social control only natural possession is recognized, and interference with natural possession is not distinguished from interference with the person or injury to the honor of the one whose physical contact with the physical object is meddled with. In the earlier legal social control the all-important thing is seisin, or possession. This is a juristic possession, a conception both of fact and of law. Such institutions as tortious conveyance by the person seised in the common law are numerous in an early stage of legal development. They show that primarily the law protected the relation to an object of one who had possession of it. Indeed the idea of *dominium*, or ownership as we now understand it, was first worked out thoroughly in Roman law, and other systems got their idea of it, as distinguished from seisin, from the Roman books.

Recognition of individual interests of substance, or in other words individual property, has developed out of recognition of group interests, just as recognition of individual interests of personality has evolved gradually from what in the first instance was a recognition of group interests. The statement which used to be found in the books that all property originally was owned in common means nothing more than this: When interests of substance are first secured they are interests of groups of kindred because in tribally organized society groups of kindred are the legal units. Social control secures these groups in the occupation of things which they have reduced to their possession. In this sense the first property is group property rather than individual property. Yet it must be noted that wherever we find a securing of group interests, the group in occupation is secured against interference of other groups with that occupation. Two ideas gradually operated to break up these group interests and bring about recognition of individual interests. One of these is the partition of households. The other is the idea of what in the Hindu law is called self-acquired property.

In primitive or archaic society as households grow unwieldy there is a partition which involves partition of property as well as of the household. Indeed in Hindu law partition is thought of as partition of the household primarily and as partition of property only incidentally. Also in Roman law the old action for partition is called the action for partitioning the household. Thus, at first, partition is a splitting up of an overgrown household into smaller households. Presently, however, it tends to become a division of a household among individuals. Thus in Roman law on the death of the head of a household each of his sons in his power at his death became a *pater familias* and could bring a proceeding to partition the inheritance although he might be the sole member of the household of which he was the head. In this way individual ownership became the normal condition instead of household ownership. In Hindu law household ownership is still regarded as the normal condition. But with changes in society and the rise of commercial and industrial activity a change has been taking place rapidly which is making individual ownership the normal type in fact, if not in legal theory.

Self-acquired property, the second disintegrating agency, may be seen in Hindu law and also in Roman law. In Hindu law all property is normally and *prima facie* household property. The burden is upon anyone who claims to be the individual owner of anything. But an exceptional class of property is recognized which is called self-acquired property. Such property might be acquired by "valor," that is, by leaving the household and going into military service and thus earning or acquiring by way of booty; or by "learning," that is, by withdrawing from the household and devoting oneself to study and thus acquiring through the gifts of the pious or the exercise of knowledge. A third form was recognized later, namely, property acquired through the use of self-acquired property. In the same way in Roman law the son in the household, even if of full age, normally had no property. Legally all property acquired by any member of the household was the property of the head of the household as the legal symbol and representative thereof. Later the head of the household ceases to be thought of as symbolizing the household and the property was regarded legally as his individual property. But Roman law recognized certain kinds of property which sons in the household might hold as their own. The first of these was property earned or acquired by the son in military service. Later property earned in the service of the state was added. Finally it came to be law that property acquired otherwise than through use of the patrimony of the household might be held by the son individually though he remained legally under the power of the head.

In the two ways just explained, through partition and through the idea of self-acquired property, individual interests in property came to be recognized throughout the law.

Except for the institution of community property between husband and wife in civil-law countries, or as it is called the matrimonial property regime, there is practically nothing left of the old system of recognized group interests. And even this remnant of household group ownership is dissolving. All legally recognized interests of substance in developed legal systems are normally individual interests. To the historical jurist of the nineteenth century this fact, coupled with the development of ownership out of possession, served to show us the idea which was realizing in human experience of the administration of justice and to confirm the position reached by the metaphysical jurists. Individual private property was a corollary of liberty and hence law was not thinkable without it. Even if we do not adopt the metaphysical part of this argument and if we give over the idealistic-political interpretation of legal history which it involves, there is much which is attractive in the theory of the historical jurists of the last century. Yet as we look at certain movements in the law there are things to give us pause. For one thing, the rise and growth of ideas of "negotiability," the development of the maxim *possession vaut titre* in continental law, and the cutting down in other ways of the sphere of recognition of the interest of the owner in view of the exigencies of the social interest in the security of transactions suggest that the tendency involved in the first of the two propositions relied on by the historical school has passed its meridian. The Roman doctrine that no one may transfer a greater title than he has is continually giving way before the demand for securing of business transactions had in good faith. And in Roman law in its maturity the rules that restricted acquisition by adverse possession and enabled the owner in many cases to reclaim after any lapse of time were superseded by a decisive limitation of actions which cut off all claims. The modern law in countries which take their law from Rome has developed this decisive limitation. Likewise in our law the hostility to the statute of limitations, so marked in eighteenth-century decisions, has given way to a policy of upholding it. Moreover the rapid rise in recent times of limitations upon the *ius disponendi*, the imposition of restrictions in order to secure the social interest in the conservation of natural resources, and English projects for cutting off the *ius abutendi* of the landowner could be interpreted by the nineteenth-century historical jurists only as marking a retrograde development. When we add that with the increase in number and influence of groups in the highly organized society of today a tendency is manifest to recognize practically and in backhanded ways group property in what are not legal entities, it becomes evident that the segment of experience at which the historical jurists were looking was far too short to justify a dogmatic conclusion, even admitting the validity of their method.

It remains to consider some twentieth-century theories. These have not been worked out with the same elaboration and systematic detail as those of the past, and as yet one may do no more than sketch them.

An instinctive claim to control natural objects is an individual interest of which the law must take account. This instinct has been the basis of psychological theories of private property. But thus far these theories have been no more than indicated. They might well be combined with the historical theory, putting a psychological basis in place of the nineteenth-century metaphysical foundation. A social-psychological legal history might achieve much in this connection.

Soviet jurists now regard ownership as a permanent institution of human society. They admit that the law must recognize property. But there is to be socialist ownership on the one hand and individual ownership on the other hand.

The distinction is said to go upon a principle of state ownership of the instruments and means of production and individual ownership of consumer's goods. This principle, however, is not consistently carried out in the Soviet law of
property. The term "consumer's goods" by no means covers
all the things which individuals are allowed to own. As Gsovski puts it, "the theory of ownership in consumer's goods,
offered as an explanation of the Soviet 'personal' ownership,
is more a slogan of economic policy than an operative legal
principle." As yet the Soviet jurists have not given us a philosophical account of their present doctrine.

Of sociological theories, some are positivist, some psychological, and some social-utilitarian. An excellent example of
the first is Duguit's deduction from social interdependence
through similarity of interest and through division of labor.
He has but sketched this theory, but his discussion contains
many valuable suggestions. He shows clearly enough that the
law of property is becoming socialized. But, as he points out,
this does not mean that property is becoming collective.
It means that we are ceasing to think of it in terms of private
right and are thinking of it in terms of social function. If one
doubts this he should reflect on recent rent legislation, which
in effect treats the renting of houses as a business affected
with a public interest in which reasonable rates must be
charged as by a public utility. Also it means that cases of legal
application of wealth to collective uses are becoming continually more numerous. He then argues that the law of
property answers to the economic need of applying certain
wealth to definite individual or collective uses and the consequent need that society guarantee and protect that application. Hence, he says, society sanctions acts which conform to
those uses of wealth which meet that economic need, and restrains acts of contrary tendency. Thus property is a social
institution based upon an economic need in a society organ-

ized through division of labor. It will be seen that the results and the attitude toward the law of property involved are much the same as those which are reached from the social-utilitarian standpoint.

Psychological sociological theories have been advanced chiefly in Italy. They seek the foundation of property in an instinct of acquisitiveness, considering it a social development or social institution on that basis.

Social-utilitarian theories explain and justify property as an institution which secures a maximum of interests or satisfies a maximum of wants, conceiving it to be a sound and wise bit of social engineering when viewed with reference to its results. This is the method of Professor Ely's well-known book, *Property and Contract*.

Recent social-economic theory has turned to the function of property in the social-welfare state. It is laid down that ownership, an absolute power of disposing of a thing, had originally been a just and adequate legal institution in a society in which property, work, and use went together in a simple economic order. Marx urged that in the evolution of society ownership of a complex of things no longer coincides with personal work and use, but as absolute control of the complex, thought of as capital, becomes a source of a power of command. Renner has developed the thesis that the juristic conception is the same but its function has changed. The owner can use his control of certain things to control other persons. So while in legal form property is an institution of private law, a complete power of doing what one likes with the thing owned, it has become in economic effect an institution of public law in the sense of a power of command exercised through incidental legal institutions developed from the law of obligations. But as Friedmann has pointed out, in the economic order of today ownership and control have become increasingly divorced. What has been called "the managerial revolution" must be taken into account. Marx's idea of technical legal ownership is not a picture of the actual situation. The part which ownership plays in the concentration of power against which men have always struggled must be appraised in a theory of property, and determination and appraisal are by no means so simple a task as jurists have assumed.

No one has done so, but I suspect one might combine the social-utilitarian and a modified economic-functional mode of thought with the civilization interpretation of the Neo-Hegelians and argue that the system of individual property, on the whole, conduces to the maintaining and furthering of civilization—to the development of human powers to the most of which they are capable—instead of viewing it as a realization of the idea of civilization as it unfolds in human experience. Perhaps the theories of the immediate future may run along some such lines. For we have had no experience of conducting civilized society on any other basis, and the waste and friction involved in going to any other basis must give us pause. Moreover, whatever we do, we must take account of the instinct of acquisitiveness and of individual claims grounded thereon. We may believe that the law of property is a wise bit of social engineering in the world as we know it, and that we satisfy more human wants, secure more interests, with a sacrifice of less thereby than by anything we are likely to devise—we may believe this without holding that private property is eternally and absolutely necessary and that human society may not conceivably expect in some civilization, which we cannot forecast, to achieve something different and something better.

CHAPTER 6

Contract

WEALTH, in a commercial age, is made up largely of promises. An important part of everyone's substance consists of advantages which others have promised to provide for or to render to him; of demands to have the advantages promised, which he may assert not against the world at large but against particular individuals. Thus the individual claims to have performance of advantageous promises secured to him. He claims the satisfaction of expectations created by promises and agreements. If this claim is not secured friction and waste obviously result, and unless some countervailing interest must come into account which would be sacrificed in the process, it would seem that the individual interest in promised advantages should be secured to the full extent of what has been assured to him by the deliberate promise of another. Let us put this in another way. In an earlier chapter I suggested, as a jural postulate of civilized society, that in such a society men must be able to assume that those with whom they deal in the general intercouse of the society will act in good faith, and as a corollary must be able to assume that those with whom they so deal will carry out their undertakings according to the expectations which the moral sentiment of the community attaches thereto. Hence in a commercial and industrial society, a claim or want or demand of society that promises be kept and that undertakings be carried out in good faith, a social interest in the stability of promises as a social and economic institution, becomes of the first importance. This social interest in the security of transactions, as one might call it, requires that we secure the individual interest of the promisee, that is, his claim or demand to be assured in the expectation created, which has become part of his substance.

In civil-law countries the interest of the promisee, and thus the social interest in the security of transactions, is secured to cover promises generally. The traditional requirement of a *causa ciuilis*, a civil, i.e., legal, reason for enforcing a pact, gave way before the teaching of the church that promises ought to be kept and the enforcement of promises as such in the canon law reinforced by natural-law ideas in the eighteenth century. Pothier gave over the contract categories of the Roman law as being "very remote from simplicity." Then came the rise of the will theory of legal transactions in the nineteenth century. French law made intention of gratuitously benefiting another a *causa*. The Austrian code of 1811 presumed a *causa*, requiring a promisor to prove there was none. And this means that he must prove the promise was not a legal transaction—that there was no intention to enter into a binding undertaking. In the result, abstract promises, as the civilian calls them, came to be enforced equally with those which came under some formal Roman category and with those having a substantial presupposition. Modern continental law, apart from certain requirements of proof, resting on the same policy as our Statute of Frauds, asks only, Did the promisor intend to create a binding duty?

Likewise in civil-law countries the enforcing machinery is modern and adequate. The oldest method of enforcement in Roman law was seizure of the person, to coerce satisfaction or hold the promisor in bondage until his kinsmen performed the judgment. Later there was a pecuniary condemnation or, as we should say, a money judgment in all cases, enforced in the classical law by universal execution or, as we should say, by involuntary bankruptcy. But along with this remedy specific relief grew up in the *actio arbitraria*, a clumsy device of specific performance on the alternative of a heavy money condemnation, which repeated itself in Pennsylvania before equity powers were given the courts, and is substantially repeating in our federal courts in their attempts to apply equitable relief to torts committed in foreign jurisdictions. The civil law developed, or perhaps the canon law developed and the civil law took over, an *actio ad implendum* or action to require performance, with natural execution, that is, a doing by the court or its officers at the expense of the defendant, of that to which he is bound as ascertained by the judgment.

As to the extent to which the individual interest in promised advantages is secured legally today, it may be said, in general, that while where the civil law prevails as the basis of the legal system there is full legal efficacy of promises and agreements intended to create obligation, the means of enforcement fall short of full securing of the interest because of lack of means of direct coercion applied to the person of a recalcitrant promisor. Where the Anglo-American common law prevails, on the other hand, while we do not attribute legal efficacy to all intentional promises intended to bind the promisor, now that we have been developing fully in many jurisdictions what the civilians call natural execution, that is, doing at the expense of the promisor what he ought but refuses to do, we have a more complete and adequate enforcing machinery in the power of courts of equity to commit for contempt of an order or decree. Also we do not grant specific relief ordinarily but only exceptionally where substituted relief (money damages) is held inadequate. On the other hand it is only where for some reason specific relief is impracticable or inadequate that the civil-law system awards damages. The civil law has the better idea at this point. But, as said above, it has no means of making its specific relief complete. The common law limits specific relief too narrowly. Moreover by taking over natural execution and through some statutory procedures of that sort, added to their original weapon of contempt proceedings, our courts of equity to the extent that they have the power to award specific relief can now make it complete and effective.

If we look into the reasons for this wide enforcement of promises in the one system and narrower enforcement in the other, we come in both cases upon a mixture of historical background and philosophical reasoning, each influencing the other and neither governing the subject completely. Philosophical theories have arisen to explain existing rules and have been the basis of new rules and of remaking of old ones. But they have been the means also, at times, of intrenching the rules they sought to explain and of fastening on the law doctrines of which it were better rid. Nowhere is the reciprocal action of legal rules and philosophical theories more strikingly manifest than in our law of contractual liability.

Law did not concern itself at first with agreements or breaches of agreements. Its function was to keep the peace by regulating or preventing private war and this only required it to deal with personal violence and with disputes over the possession of property. I may remind you of the proposition of Hippodamus in the fifth century B.C. that there were but three subjects of lawsuits, namely, insult, injury, and homicide. If a dispute over breach of an agreement led to an assault and a breach of the peace, tribunals might be called on to act. But it was the assault not the breach of agreement with which they were concerned. Controversy as to possession of property was a fertile source of disturbance of the peace and tribunals would entertain an action to recover possession. Agreements to compound for a wrong are perhaps the earliest type. But the law had its eye upon the need of composition, not upon the agreement. No basis for a law of contracts was to be found in the power of the tribunals with respect to injuries although our law did make assumpsit out of trespass on the case. On the other hand, recovery of property could be used for this purpose. Hence the first legal, as distinguished from religious, contract was worked out on the analogy of a real transaction. Before this, however, another possibility had developed in the religiously sanctioned promise.

Religion, the internal discipline of the organized kindred, and the law of the state were three co-ordinate agencies of social control in ancient society. Nor was law for a long time the chief of these nor the one which covered the widest field. If the gods had been called to witness or good faith had a religious sanction, the duty to keep a promise was a matter for religion. Otherwise the mere pact or agreement not within the cognizance of the priests was but a matter for self-help. Hindu law shows the idea of religious duty to keep faith in full vigor. In the Hindu system the relation between the parties to a debt is not legal but religious and after law had grown up under English influence it was said that there is a legal obligation because there is a religious obligation. A man is bound in law because and to the extent that he is bound in religion and not otherwise and no more. To the Hindu lawyer a debt is not an obligation merely. It is a sin the consequences whereof follow the debtor into another world. Brihaspati says: "He who, having received a sum lent or the like does not return it to the owner, will be born hereafter in his creditor's house a slave, a servant, a woman or a quadruped." Narada says that when one dies without having paid his debt, "the whole merit of his devotions or of his perpetual fire belongs to his creditors." In short the debtor is looked on as one who wrongfully withholds from the creditor the latter's property and hence as in some sort a thief. The legal idea, so far as there is one, is not one of obligation but of a property right in the creditor. One may suspect that religious obligation arising from the detention of property is a legal way of putting it in a polity in which social control is primarily religious and religious precepts are turning into legal precepts. At any rate the Hindus carry the idea of religious obligation so far that a descendant is bound to pay the debts of his ancestor in many cases whether he receives any assets of the ancestor or not. The liability of the son to pay the father's debt is held to arise from the moral and religious duty of rescuing the father from the penalties attaching in a future state to nonpayment of debts. Accordingly if the debt is of such a kind that no penalties would so attach, there is no religious duty and hence no obligation imposed upon the descendant.

Roman law in its earliest stage was not unlike this. Agreements of themselves were not cognizable by the tribunals. It was no ground for summoning a defendant before the magistrate that he had made a promise and had broken it. Agreements were matters for religion or for kin or guild discipline. If one had called on the gods to witness his promise or sworn to fulfill it, he was liable to pontifical discipline. The presence of an impious oath breaker was a social danger and he might be devoted to the infernal gods. As law replaced religion as the controlling regulative agency, the old religiously sanctioned promise becomes a formal legal contract. Thus in the strict law we get formal contracts with their historical origin in religious duty, and formal contracts with their historical origin in a legal duty created by a real transaction of suretyship or conveyance, perhaps by calling the people to witness so that there is an affront to the state if they are called upon in vain.

When contact with Greek philosophers set the Roman

jurists to thinking about the basis of obligation there were two sorts of promises: (1) Formal promises, (a) by stipulation, using the sacramental word *spondeo* and thus assuming the pouring out of a libation that the gods might take notice of the promise, (b) by public ceremony apparently symbolizing a real transaction before the whole people, (c) entered upon the household books of account; and (2) mere informal promises not recognized by law. The latter depended wholly on the good faith of the maker since the law had put down self-help which formerly had been available to the promisee. Accordingly Roman jurists distinguished civil obligations and natural obligations—those recognized and secured legally and those which primarily had only a moral efficacy. A *nudum pactum* or mere agreement or mere promise, not clothed with legal efficacy because it did not come within any of the categories of legal transactions sanctioned by the *ius ciuile*, created only a natural obligation. It was right and just to adhere to such a pact, but only contracts, undertakings recognized by law because of their form or nature, were enforceable.

With increasing pressure of the social interest in the security of transactions through economic development and commercial expansion, the natural-law philosophy slowly affected this simple scheme of formal undertakings legally recognized and enforceable and informal undertakings of only moral efficacy, and brought about the complicated system of enforceable undertakings in the maturity of Roman law with which you are familiar. Four features of this movement are noteworthy. In the first place it led to a juristic theory of formal contract which has affected our ideas ever since. In the strict law the source of obligation was in the form itself. For in primitive thinking forms have an intrinsic efficacy. It has often been pointed out that the faith in legal forms belongs to the same order of thought as faith in forms of incantation, and that legal forms are frequently symbols to be classed psychologically with the symbols of magic. The stage of equity and natural law, relying on reason rather than on form, governed by philosophy instead of by naïve faith, looked for the substance and found it in a pact preceding and presupposed by the formal ceremony. Thus a formal contract was a pact with the addition of legal form. The pact was the substance of the transaction. The form was a *causa ciuilis* or legal reason for enforcing the pact. But if the form was only a legal reason for enforcing something that got its natural efficacy in another way, it followed that there might well be other legal reasons for enforcement besides form. Consequently new categories of contract were added to the old formal contracts, and it is significant that while the latter were transactions *stricti iuris* the former were considered transactions *bonae fidei* involving liability to what good faith demanded in view of what had been done. In the scope of their obligation these contracts responded exactly to the postulate of civilized society that those with whom we deal will act in good faith and will carry out their undertakings according to the expectations of the community. On the other hand, the old formal contracts responded thereto in part only since their obligation was one to do exactly what the terms of the form called for, no more and no less. When one makes *nexum*, said the Twelve Tables, as he says orally, so be the law. New categories were added in successive strata, as it were, and juristic science sought afterward to reduce them to system and logical consistency. Thus real contracts, consensual contracts, and innominate contracts were added. But it is evident that many of these are juristic rationalizings of what had been done for a long time through formal transactions. Thus the consensual contract of sale with its implied warranties rationalizes transfer by *traditio* with stipulations for the price and for warranties. The real contract of *depositum* rationalizes *fiducia cum amico*. The real contract of *mutuum* rationalizes *pecunia credita*. But the latter was so thoroughly established as a formal transaction that the case of a loan of money, analytically a real contract, preserved the incidents of the strict law. Moreover certain pacts, *pacta adiecta*, *pacta praetoria*, became actionable which do not fit into the analytical scheme of the Institutes. For example, a *causa* or reason for enforcing these pacts was found in their being incidental to something else or in a pre-existing natural obligation which they undertook to satisfy. There still remained natural obligations which had not been given legal efficacy as the basis of actions. The mere will of the person who undertook or the claim of the promisee was not a reason for enforcing. Yet in reason they were morally binding and the legal and moral should coincide. Hence they might be used defensively or as the basis of a setoff. Meanwhile the forms of stipulation and of literal contract had been reduced to their lowest terms by conceiving them in terms of substance, and taking orally expressed agreement to be the substance of the one and writing to be the substance of the other. The results have defied analysis although the best that juristic ingenuity could do has been expended upon them for centuries.

In the Middle Ages primitive ideas came back for a time through Germanic law. General security in its lowest terms of peace and order was the pressing social interest. There was little commercial activity. The civilization of the time did not involve the corollaries of our jural postulate. Religiously sanctioned undertakings by promissory oath and real transactions of pledge of person or property and of exchange gave rise to a simple system of formal undertakings. Out of these came a theory of *causa debendi*, or reason for owing the promised performance, which has had a profound influence upon subsequent thinking. The Roman *causa ciuilis* was a legal reason for enforcing a pact. Under the influence of the Germanic idea *causa* becomes a reason for making the pact, the good reason for making it furnishing a sufficient reason for enforcing it. For a time it seemed that the church might succeed in establishing a jurisdiction over promises. Oaths and vows involved religious duties and might well be claimed as the province of the spiritual. But the moral obligation of pacts, binding the conscience of a Christian, might also be cognizable by a zealous corrector of the conduct of the faithful for their souls' welfare. Had not the power of the canon law broken down and the law of the state developed rapidly in respect of the security of transactions after the sixteenth century, the law of contracts might have grown along religious instead of along philosophical lines, and perhaps not to its advantage. As it is, one need but read Doctor and Student with the title *de pactis* of the *Corpus Iuris Canonici* and casuist writings as to the moral efficacy of promises before him to see that religion paved the way for much that was done presently in the name of philosophy.

To the jurists of the seventeenth and eighteenth centuries no distinction between natural obligation and civil obligations was maintainable, since all natural rights or obligations must for the very reason that they were natural be legal also. If it was morally obligatory that one adhere to a pact, then it must be treated as a contract. However much systematized analytically, the Roman categories of contract did not deal with undertakings from this standpoint. What the jurists desired was not analytical categories but a principle upon which men were to be held or not to be held upon their promises. Thus the philosophy of contract, the principles underlying the binding force of promises and agreements, became the chief problem of philosophical jurisprudence of the seventeenth century, as interests of personality were the chief subject of discussion in the eighteenth century, and interests of substance, the philosophy of the law of property, the chief subject of discussion in the nineteenth century. The decisive element in seventeenth-century thought as to contract was the idea of natural law; the idea of deduction from the nature of man as a moral creature and of legal rules and legal institutions which expressed this ideal of human nature. But the idea was put to work upon existing materials and the result was a reciprocal influence of the conception of enforcing promises as such because morally binding, on the one hand, shaped to some extent by canon law and casuist discussions of what promises were binding in conscience and when, and the ideas of *nudum pactum* and *causa debendi*, on the other hand. Roman law was assumed to be embodied reason. As D'Aguesseau put it, Rome was ruling by her reason, having ceased to rule by her authority. Hence all consideration of the subject starts with the assumption that there are morally naked agreements which for that reason are to be naked legally. Where there was an exchange of promises there was the authority of Justinian for enforcement (*synallagma*), and it was easy to find a reason in the analogy of exchange of property. Where something was exchanged for a promise, that something was a *causa debendi*. But suppose there was no exchange of promises nor was anything exchanged for the promise. There was nothing but a promise assented to. In Roman law this would have to take the form of a stipulation. In the Germanic law it would have required an oath or the form of a real transaction of pledge or exchange. At common law it required delivery of a sealed instrument. Clearly there was no moral efficacy inherent in these forms. Why should these "abstract" promises be enforced and not others? Should every such promise be enforced or should none be enforced without something in the way of exchange, or should such promises be classified for the purpose of enforcement, and if so, how?

Two theories arose in the seventeenth century. One may be called the theory of an equivalent. This theory is obviously a rationalization of the Germanic *causa debendi* influenced by canon law and casuist writings. According to this theory an abstract promise, no equivalent having been given for it, is not naturally and hence is not legally binding. Three reasons have been given for this which have figured in juristic discussion of the subject ever since. It was said that one who trusts another who makes a promise for no equivalent does so rashly. He cannot ask to be secured in such an unfounded expectation. This is too much in the spirit of the strict law. It denies any interest except where the law secures it. It says that if the law does not secure the interest, one is a fool to rely on the promise and so has no interest. In like manner the strict law said that if one gave his formal undertaking through fraud or mistake or coercion, he was a fool or a coward and was not to be helped. But we cannot prove the interest by the law. We must measure the law with reference to the interest. Again it was said that if one promises without equivalent he does so more from "ostentation" than from real intention and so an equivalent shows that he acted from calculation and deliberately. It is only deliberate promises that are morally binding, for only such promises are relied upon by the prudent, upright man in his intercourse with his neighbors. If this reason is sound, equivalent is only a mode of proving deliberation and the real point should be that the promise was made deliberately as something by which the maker expected to be bound, not that the deliberation was evidenced in a particular way by an equivalent. A third reason was that one who parted with an equivalent in exchange for or in reliance on a promise is injured in his substance if the promise is not kept. But if this is the reason, the law should simply require restitution in case of nonperformance. If the interest involved is the deduction from substance through rendering the equivalent, the obligation should be *quasi ex contractu* rather than *ex contractu*.

Our Anglo-American law of contracts was much influenced by this theory of equivalents. In the seventeenth century four types of promise were legally enforceable at common law: (1) A formal acknowledgment of indebtedness by bond under seal, often conditioned upon performance of a promise for which it was a security; (2) a covenant or undertaking under seal; (3) the real contract of debt; and (4) a simple promise upon consideration, that is, in exchange for an act or for another promise. The first conclusively acknowledged an equivalent, in the second it could be said that the seal presupposed or implied one, in the third the obligation arose from the detention of something by him to whom it had been delivered, and in the fourth the act or counterpromise was the motive or consideration for the promise and as a cause of or reason for making it was the equivalent for which the promisor chose to assume the undertaking. With some aid from a dogmatic fiction in the case of covenants, the common law could be adjusted to this theory reasonably well. Accordingly as far back as Bacon we find consideration treated from this standpoint in the English books. But it was never a satisfactory explanation. If the theory was sound it ought not to matter whether the equivalent was rendered before the promise or after it or simultaneously with it. Indeed, English equity in the nineteenth century took subsequent action in reliance upon a promise of a gift to be a common-law consideration on the basis whereof the promise was specifically enforceable. Equity never wholly adopted this or any other theory. At least after the middle of the eighteenth century equity was supposed to follow the law as to what was a contract. But the common law was not settled till the nineteenth century, and we find the chancellors using consideration frequently to mean not equivalent but any reason for making the promise and thus making it synonymous with the civilian's *causa*. The so-called meritorious consideration, consideration of blood and of love and affection, and the cases of promises sustained by moral obligation of a debtor to secure his creditor, of a husband to settle property on his wife, and of a parent to provide for a child show the idea of *causa* at work in equity. It is significant that Doctor and Student was often cited in these connections. The most thoroughgoing attempt to apply the equivalent theory to be found in the books is Langdell's working out of a system of the so-called conditions implied in law or dependent promises on that basis. As an example of vigorous legal analysis it rivals Austin. But it did not succeed in shaping the law.

On the Continent the second theory, the theory of the inherent moral force of a promise made as such, came to prevail. This was the theory of Grotius. It was generally adopted by continental writers of the eighteenth century and, as has been seen, it broke down the Roman categories and led to the rule that a promise as such, intending a legal transaction, created legal obligation. At the end of the eighteenth century Lord Mansfield came very near establishing it in our law by his doctrine that no promise made as a business transaction could be *nudum pactum*. But he was too late. Growth stopped for a season and the nineteenth century set itself to systematize and harmonize what it had received rather than to carry the development further.

When the natural-law foundation of enforcing promises crumbled, the metaphysical jurists sought to provide a new one. Kant said that it was impossible to prove that one ought to keep his promise, considered merely as a promise, and deduced contract from property as a form of conveyance or alienation of one's substance involved in the very idea of individual rights. So far as consistent with abstract freedom of will according to a universal law, one might alienate his services as well as his property, and an undertaking to perform something was an alienation of that sort. This view was generally taken, so that while the seventeenth century sought to rest rights upon contract and the eighteenth century rested contract on the inherent moral significance of a promise, the nineteenth century, making the philosophy of property the important thing, rested contract on property. Three of these theories are worth a moment's notice.

Fichte says that the duty of performing an agreement arises when one party thereto begins to act under it. Juristically this seems to be a rationalization of the Roman innominate contract. There, in case a pact was performed on one side, he who performed might claim restitution *quasi ex contractu* or claim the counter-performance *ex contractu*. Philosophically the idea seems to be that of the equivalent theory, in the form with which we are familiar in Anglo-American discussion of this subject as the injurious-reliance theory. According to the latter, unless the promisee has parted with an equivalent or has begun to act in reliance upon the agreement, he has no moral claim to fulfillment. This is not a theory of the law as it is or as it ever has been. Formal contracts require nothing of the sort. It is true, English equity, under the influence of the equivalent theory, did lay down in the nineteenth century that a contract under seal with no common-law consideration behind it would not be enforced. But that proposition was subject to many exceptions when it was announced, more have since developed and more are developing. As things are, the exceptions are of more frequent application than the rule itself. Nor is Fichte's theory a statement of moral ideas of his day or of ours. Then and now the moral duty to keep abstract promises was and is recognized. That a man's word should be "as good as his bond" expresses the moral sentiment of civilized society. But the philosopher saw that the law did not go so far and was trying to frame a rational explanation of why it fell short. It should be noticed that Fichte is really trying to show why a promise may be regarded as a part of one's substance and why one's claim to performance may be treated as his property.

Hegel also explains contract in terms of property, treating a promise as a disposition of one's substance. Hence in his view the so-called abstract promise is a mere subjective qualification of one's will which he is at liberty to change. This theory and the foregoing assume the Roman law or the older law of continental Europe, and speak from the reaction from natural law which in England at the same time was overruling the liberal doctrines of Lord Mansfield.

Later metaphysical jurists rely upon the idea of personality. The Romanist thinks of a legal transaction as a willing of some change in a person's sphere of rights to which the law, carrying out his will, gives the intended effect. If the transaction is executed, revocation would involve aggression upon the substance of another. If it is executory, however, why should the declared intent that the change take place in the future be executed by law despite the altered will of the promisor? Some say that this should be done where there is a joint will from which only joint action may recede. Where the parties have come to an agreement, where their wills have been at one, the law is to give effect to this joint will as a sort of vindication of personality. It is evident, however, that this explanation assumes the will theory, the subjective theory of legal transactions. If we start from the objective theory it breaks down. Take for instance the case of an offer, which a reasonable man would understand in a given way, accepted by the offeree in that understanding when the offeror really meant something else. Or take the case of an offer wrongly transmitted by telegraph and accepted in good faith as it is transmitted. Here there is no community of will and yet the law may well hold, as we do in America, in both cases, that there is a contract. No metaphysical theory has prevailed to prevent the steady march of the law and of juristic thought in the direction of an objective doctrine of legal transactions. Nowhere, indeed, has the deductive method broken down so completely as in the attempt to deduce principles upon which contracts are to be enforced.

Later in the nineteenth century men came to think more about freedom of contract than about enforcement of promises when made. To Spencer and the mechanical positivists conceiving of law negatively as a system of hands off while men do things, rather than as a system of ordering to prevent friction and waste so that they may do things, the important institution was a right of free exchange and free contract, deduced from the law of equal freedom as a sort of freedom of economic motion and locomotion. Justice required that each individual be at liberty to make free use of his natural powers in bargains and exchanges and promises except as he interfered with like action on the part of his fellow men, or with some other of their natural rights. Whether all such transactions should be enforced against him or only some, and if the latter, which, are questions belonging to an affirmative rather than to a negative science of law.

Historical jurists accepted the will theory and have been its leading advocates in modern times. They saw that the whole course of legal history had been one of wider recognition and more effective enforcement of promises. Those who accepted the ethical idealistic interpretation of legal history could see freedom as an ethical idea realizing itself in a larger freedom of self-assertion and self-determination through promises and agreements and a wider giving effect to the will so asserted and determined. For the most part they wrote on the Continent where the field of legally enforceable promises had ceased to be bounded by a narrow fence of Roman historical categories. Thus they had no call to rationalize dogmas of not enforcing promises made as business transactions. Those who accepted the political interpretation saw freedom as a civil or political idea realizing itself in a progress from *status* to contract in which men's duties and liabilities came more and more to flow from willed action instead of from the accident of social position recognized by law. The English historical jurists might well have asked how far English rules as to consideration were consonant with the implications of such a theory, and whether they must not be expected to give way as the idea unfolded more completely in experience of popular action and judicial decision. But the leader of this school was not a common-law lawyer, and the American historical jurists devoted their energies to devising a historical-analytical theory of consideration rather than to the wider question of what promises should be enforced and why.

Here as in other places the historical jurist and the utilitarian were in agreement as to results although they differed widely as to the mode of reaching them. The former saw in contract a realization of the idea of liberty. The latter saw in it a means of promoting that maximum of individual free self-assertion which he took to be human happiness. Hence the former called for freedom of contract and should have called for wide general enforcement of promises. The latter held to a doctrine of unshackling men and allowing them to act as freely as possible, which involved the complementary position of extending the sphere and enforcing the obligation of contract. The difference between these ways of thinking and those of the end of the eighteenth century is brought out if we compare Blackstone (1765) with a dictum of Sir George Jessel a century later (1875). The former says that the public is "in nothing so essentially interested as in securing to every individual his private rights."

The latter, discussing a question of what agreements are against public policy and therefore unenforceable, says: "If there is one thing more than another which public policy requires it is that men of full age and competent understanding shall have the utmost liberty of contracting and that such contracts shall be enforced by courts of justice." But the utilitarians put the emphasis upon the first, the negative, rather than upon the second, the affirmative, part of this twofold program. This is true also of the historical jurists and of the positivists. The English trader and entrepreneur was not seeking for legal instruments. He could work passably with those which the law furnished if the law would but let him. What he sought was to be free from legal shackles which had come down from a society of a different nature organized on a different basis and with other ends. Hence juristic thought addressed itself to this for a season rather than to the doctrine of consideration and the reason for nonenforcement of deliberate promises where not put in the form of bargains.

No one of the four theories of enforcing promises which are current today is adequate to cover the whole legal recognition and enforcement of them as the law actually exists. Putting them in the order of their currency, we may call them (1) the will theory, (2) the bargain theory, (3) the equivalent theory, (4) the injurious-reliance theory. That is, promises are enforced as a giving effect to the will of those who agree, or to the extent that they are bargains or parts of bargains, or where an equivalent for them has been rendered, or where they have been relied on by the promisee to his injury, according to the theory chosen. The first has been the prevailing theory among civilians. But it must give way before the onward march of the objective theory of legal transactions and is already fighting a rear-guard action. In our law it is impossible. We do not give effect to promises on the

basis of the will of the promisor, although our courts of
equity have shown some tendency to move in that direction.
The attempt in the nineteenth century to Romanize our
theories of liability involved a Romanized will theory of contract. But no one who looks beneath the surface of our law
reports can doubt that the attempt has failed wholly. We
no longer seek solutions on every side through a pedantic
Romanized law of bailments, and in the law of bailments itself we are coming to talk in common-law terms of negligence in view of the circumstances and not in Romanist
terms of the willed standard of diligence and corresponding
degrees of negligence. In America, at least, the objective theory of contract is orthodox and the leader of English analytical jurists of the present generation has expounded it
zealously. Courts of equity, which inherit modes of thought
from the time when the chancellor searched the conscience
of a defendant by an examination under oath and believed he
could reach subjective data that were beyond the cognizance
of a jury, are the last stronghold of the exotic subjective
theory in the common law.

Probably the bargain theory is the one most current in
common-law thinking. It is a development of the equivalent
theory. It will not cover formal contracts but under its influence the formal contracts have been slowly giving way.
The seal "imports" a consideration. Legislation has abolished
it in many jurisdictions and often it does no more than establish a bargain *prima facie*, subject to proof that there was in
fact no consideration. Courts of equity require a common-
law consideration, at least on the face of their general rule,
before they will enforce a sealed contract. Also the formal
contracts of the law merchant are subject to defeat by showing there was no consideration, except when in the hands of
holders for value without notice. Here, however, consideration is used in the sense of equivalent, to the extent of ad-

mitting a "past consideration," and the bargain theory, appropriate to simple contracts, is not of entire application. On the other hand, the extent to which courts today are straining to get away from the bargain theory and enforce promises which are not bargains and cannot be stated as such is significant. Subscription contracts, gratuitous promises afterward acted on, promises based on moral obligations, new promises where a debt has been barred by limitation or bankruptcy or the like, the torturing of gifts into contracts by equity so as to enforce *pacta donationis* specifically in spite of the rule that equity will not aid a volunteer, the enforcement of gratuitous declarations of trust, specific enforcement of options under seal without consideration, specific performance by way of reformation in case of security to a creditor or settlement on a wife or provision for a child, voluntary relinquishment of a defense by a surety and other cases of "waiver," release by mere acknowledgment in some states, enforcement of gifts by way of reformation against the heir of a donor, "mandates" where there is no *res*, and stipulations of parties and their counsel as to the conduct of and proceedings in litigation—all these make up a formidable catalogue of exceptional or anomalous cases with which the advocate of the bargain theory must struggle. When one adds enforcement of promises at suit of third-party beneficiaries, which is making headway the world over, and enforcement of promises where the consideration moves from a third person, which has strong advocates in America and is likely to be used to meet the exigencies of doing business through letters of credit, one can but see that Lord Mansfield's proposition that no promise made as a business transaction can be *nudum pactum* is nearer realization than we had supposed.

Yet the equivalent theory and the injurious-reliance theory are even less adequate to explain the actual law. The equiva-

lent theory must wrestle at the outset with the doctrine that
inadequacy of consideration is immaterial so that the equiva-
lency is often Pickwickian. Hegel could argue for it on the
basis of the Roman *laesio enormis*. But when a court of equity
is willing to uphold a sale of property worth $20,000 for $200,
even a dogmatic fiction is strained. Moreover the catalogue
of anomalies with which the bargain theory must wrestle
contains more than one difficulty for the adherent of either
theory. Stipulations in the course of litigation do not need
equivalents nor do they need to be acted on in order to be
enforceable. A release by mere acknowledgment, when good
at all, needs no equivalent and need not be acted on. Waiver
by a surety of the defense of release by giving time to the
principal needs no element of consideration nor of estoppel.
Defectively executed securities, settlements, and advance-
ments need no equivalent and need not be acted on in order
to be reformed. Options under seal are held open in equity on
the basis of the seal alone. A gratuitously declared trust
creates an obligation cognizable in equity without more. In
truth the situation in our law is becoming much the same
as that in the maturity of Roman law and for the same reason. We have three main categories. First, there are formal
contracts, including sealed instruments, recognizances, and
the formal contracts of the law merchant, in which latter the
form consists in the use of certain words, requirements as to
sum certain, payment at all events, and certainty as to time.
Second, there are the real contracts of debt and bailment.
Third, there are simple contracts, without form and upon
consideration. The latter is the growing category although
the formal contracts of the law merchant have shown some
power of growth and the business world has been trying to
add thereto letters of credit using the formal words "con-
firmed" or "irrevocable." But the category of enforceable
simple promises defies systematic treatment as obstinately

as the actionable pacts in Roman law. Successive additions at different times in the endeavor of courts to hold men to their undertakings, in view of the social interest in the security of transactions and the jural postulates of the civilization of the day, proceed on all manner of different theories and different analogies and agree only in the result—that a man's word in the course of business should be as good as his bond and that his fellow men must be able to rely on the one equally with the other if our economic order is to function efficiently. It is evident that many courts consciously or subconsciously sympathize with Lord Dunedin's feeling that one can have no liking for a doctrine which enables a promisor to snap his fingers at a promise deliberately made, fair in itself, and in which the person seeking to enforce it has a legitimate interest according to the ordinary understanding of upright men in the community. It is significant that although we have been theorizing about consideration for four centuries, our texts have not agreed upon a formula of consideration, much less our courts upon any consistent scheme of what is consideration and what is not. It means one thing—we are not agreed exactly what—in the law of simple contracts, another in the law of negotiable instruments, another in conveyancing under the Statute of Uses and still another thing—no one knows exactly what—in many cases in equity.

Letters of credit afford a striking illustration of the ill adaptation of our American common law of contract to the needs of modern business in an urban society of highly complex economic organization. Well known abroad and worked out consistently on general theories in the commercial law of continental Europe, these instruments came into use in this country on a large scale suddenly during the first World War. There was no settled theory with respect to them in our books and the decisions warranted four or

five views leading to divergent results in matters of vital moment to the business man who acted on them. Character-
istically the business world set out to make of them formal
contracts of the law merchant by the use of certain distinc-
tive words which gave the instruments character and made
their nature clear to those who inspected them anywhere in
the world. But for a season our category of mercantile spe-
cialties had ceased to admit of growth, and the doctrine of
consideration with its uncertain lines stood in the way of
many things which the exigencies of business called for
and business men found themselves doing in reliance on each
other's business honor and the banker's jealousy of his business credit, with or without assistance from the law. Certainly no one would say that such a situation bears witness
to wise social engineering in an economically organized society resting on credit.

Two circumstances operate to keep the requirement of
consideration alive in our law of simple contract. One is the
professional feeling that the common law is the legal order of
nature, that its doctrines in an idealized form are natural
law, and that its actual rules are declaratory of natural law.
This mode of thinking is to be found in all professions and
is a result of habitual application of the rules of an art until
they are taken for granted. In law it is fortified by the theory
of natural law which has governed in our elementary books
since Blackstone, was taught to all lawyers until the present
century, and is assumed in much of our judicial decision.
Later it was strengthened by the theories of the historical
school which ruled in our law schools in the last quarter of
the nineteenth century and taught us to think that growth
must inevitably follow lines which might be discovered in
the Year Books. These things co-operated with the temper
of the last century and the instinctive aversion of the lawyer
to change, lest in some unperceived way a door be opened to

magisterial caprice or to the personal equation of the judge. Thus some thought of consideration, whatever it was, as inherent in the very idea of enforceable promises. Others assumed that it was a historically developed principle by which the future evolution of the law of contracts must be governed. Many others simply thought that it was dangerous to talk of change. And yet change has gone on rapidly, if subconsciously, until the present confused mass of unsystematized and unsystematizable rules has resulted. The second circumstance operating to keep alive the requirement of consideration is a more legitimate factor.

Nowhere could psychology render more service to jurisprudence than in giving us a psychological theory of *nuda pacta*. For there is something more than the fetish of a traditional Latin phrase with the hallmark of Roman legal science behind our reluctance to enforce all deliberate promises simply as such. It should be compared with the reluctance of courts to apply the ordinary principle of negligence to negligent speech, with the doctrine as to seller's talk, with the limitations upon liability for oral defamation, and with many things of the sort throughout our law. All of these proceed partly from the attitude of the strict law in which our legal institutions first took shape. But they have persisted because of a feeling that "talk is cheap," that much of what men say is not to be taken at face value, and that more will be sacrificed than gained if all oral speech is taken seriously and the principles applied by the law to other forms of conduct are applied rigorously thereto. This is what was meant when the writers on natural law said that promises often proceeded more from "ostentation" than from a real intention to assume a binding relation. But this feeling may be carried too far. Undoubtedly it has been carried too far in the analogous cases above mentioned. The rule of *Derry* v. *Peek* goes much beyond what is needed to secure reasonable limits for human garrulousness. The standard of negligence, taking into account the fact of oral speech and the character and circumstances of the speech in the particular case, would amply secure individual free utterance. So also the doctrine that one might not rely on another's oral representation in the course of a business transaction, if he could ascertain the facts by diligence, went much too far and has had to be restricted. Likewise we have had to extend liability for oral defamation. Accordingly because men are prone to overmuch talk it does not follow that promises made by business men in business dealings or by others as business transactions are in any wise likely to proceed from "ostentation," or that we should hesitate to make them as binding in law as they are in business morals. Without accepting the will theory, may we not take a suggestion from it and enforce those promises which a reasonable man in the position of the promisee would believe to have been made deliberately with intent to assume a binding relation? The general security is more easily and effectively guarded against fraud by requirements of proof after the manner of the Statute of Frauds than by requirements of consideration which is as easy to establish by doubtful evidence as the promise itself. This has been demonstrated abundantly by experience of suits in equity to enforce oral contracts taken out of the Statute of Frauds by great hardship and part performance.

Revived philosophical jurisprudence has its first and perhaps its greatest opportunity in the Anglo-American law of contracts. The constantly increasing list of theoretical anomalies shows that analysis and restatement can avail us no longer. Indeed the lucid statement of Williston but emphasizes the inadequacy of analysis even when eked out by choice from among competing views and analytical restatements of judicial dogma in the light of results. Projects for "restatement of the law" are in the air. But a restatement of what has never been stated is an impossibility, and as yet there is no authoritative statement of what the law of consideration is. Nothing could be gained by a statement of it with all its imperfections on its head, and any consistent analytical statement would require the undoing of much that the judges have done quietly beneath the surface for making promises more widely enforceable. Given an attractive philosophical theory of enforcement of promises, our courts in a new period of growth will begin to shape the law thereby, and judicial empiricism and legal reason will bring about a workable system along new lines. The possibilities involved may be measured if we compare our old law of torts with its hard and fast series of nominate wrongs, its distinctions growing out of procedural requirements of trespass and trespass on the case and its crude idea of liability, flowing solely from causation, with the law of torts at the end of the nineteenth century after it had been molded by the theory of liability as a corollary of fault. Even if we must discard the conception that tort liability may flow only from fault, the generalization did a service of the first magnitude not only to legal theory but to the actual administration of justice. No less service will be rendered by the twentieth-century philosophical theory, whatever it is, which puts the jural postulate of civilized society in our day and place with respect to good faith, and its corollary as to promises, in acceptable form, and furnishes jurist and judge and lawmaker with a logical critique, a workable measure of decision, and an ideal of what the law seeks to do, whereby to carry forward the process of enlarging the domain of legally enforceable promises and thus enlarging on this side the domain of legal satisfaction of human claims.

While the law had been coming more and more and today had seemed to come almost substantially to the position of morals, that promises as such are to be kept, there is coming to be a serious cleavage in an increasing breakdown of the strict moral doctrine as to the obligation of a promise. This had been a cardinal proposition of publicists from the argument of Demosthenes that the citizen should obey the laws as common agreements and Cicero's praise of *prisca fides* in a treatise on duties; of Christian morals from the pronouncement of the Council of Carthage incorporated in the Corpus of the Canon Law and taken on therefrom by the civil law; and of writers on natural law in the seventeenth and eighteenth centuries, as witnessed by the pronouncement of Strykius that we know from Scripture that God held himself bound by a promise and that the Devil and the Prince were bound by promises also. The founders of our American constitutional democracy held that it derived its just powers from the consent of the governed. Likewise our chief American text writer on the law of contract in the nineteenth century laid down that "all rights, all duties, all obligations, and all law" grew out of promises or undertakings declared or understood. Today the Marxian economic interpretation, the rise of the service state, and the humanitarian theory of legal liability, in different ways and in varying degrees, are leading to a radically different view of the significance of a promise.

Paschukanis, the juristic and economic adviser to the Soviet government in Russia until the purge in 1936, held that law had its basis only in the exigencies of exchange of commodities, or in other words the demands of business. It made trade possible by adjusting the controversies that arise out of it. If there could be no ownership there could be no conflicting interests to be adjusted and so no need of law. His teachings have been repudiated by the present regime in Russia. The state is held to be an organization of compulsion. But the law of obligations or of contracts in the widest sense of that term, which makes up the bulk of the law in the modern codes as well as in the uncodified law of the English-speaking world, finds little real place in the Soviet system.

There has been a longer experience of the service state in continental Europe than we have had in English-speaking lands. Hence it is instructive to see how the law of contracts has been faring in France. Two phenomena of the contemporary law of contracts are discussed by French jurists. One is what Josserand calls "contractual dirigism," i.e., a regime of state making of contracts for people instead of leaving contracts to be made by the parties themselves. The other is a humanitarian idea of rendering a service to debtors or promisors by the state lifting or shifting burdens or losses, and hence the burden of promises, so as to put them upon those better able to bear them. The two are closely related. When contracts are made for people by the service state they do not feel any strong moral duty to perform them. If the state makes the contract let the state perform it or compensate the disappointed promisee. Hence we read in the French law books of today about "the principle of favor to the debtor" and Ripert speaks ironically of what he calls "the right not to pay debts."

The French Civil Code in 1804 put the obligatory force of a contract emphatically thus: "Agreements legally formed take the place of law for those who have made them." Planiol tells us that this doctrine of the obligatory force of a contract had a twofold basis: "A moral idea, respect for the given word, and economic interest, the necessity of credit." Indeed this comparison of a promise to a law was traditional. The Romans called a strict foreclosure clause in a pledge a *lex commissoria.* In the *Digest* of Justinian, Ulpian (third century) speaks of a contract as a law for the parties. Domat repeated this in the seventeenth century. The nineteenth-century metaphysical jurists, to whom freedom of the individual will was the central point in their science of law,

developed and refined it. Thus a writer on philosophy of
law in 1884 said: ". . . it is impossible in an ultimate analysis
to draw a distinction between a contract and an act of Parliament." Again he says: "In like manner the whole operation
of preparing contracts, agreements, settlements, conveyances
and such deeds, is purely legislative. The conveyancer who
prepares a contract of copartnery, or articles of association
of a company, is framing a code for a greater or smaller number of persons. A marriage settlement or a will is equivalent
to a private act of Parliament regulating the succession of
a particular person or persons. . . . All such deeds make
the law for the persons involved." In other words the free
wills of the parties had made the law for them. The courts
could no more change this than any other part of the law.
Even the legislator was bound to respect it as to the contracts of the past. That idea was put in the Constitution of
the United States. But it has been disappearing all over the
world. In France it is gone entirely. This was covered up for
a time by what Austin would have called spurious interpretation. By assuming that the will of the parties had not
been fully expressed, courts could discover in contracts
terms which were not there and were not in the minds of the
parties, and could modify the terms which they found there.
French legislation then went further and gave the judges
power to suspend or rescind contracts and change their conditions. The parties no longer made law for themselves by
free contract. French lawyers tell us that partly there was a
moral idea here. Contracts might be improvident or changes
in the economic situation might affect the value of the promised performance or of the given or promised equivalent.
This is akin to an idea we may see at work in the law of
legal liability everywhere. It is a humanitarian idea of lifting
or shifting burdens and losses so as to put them upon those

better able to bear them. Belief in the obligatory force of contracts and respect for the given word are going, if not in some spots actually gone, in the law of today

French jurists tell us that this means a shift to a state-directed economy. Planiol puts it thus. "If the state undertakes to direct the economy itself it cannot admit the maintenance of contract relations contrary to those it envisages. Contracts of long duration become impossible where in all cases they are exposed to revision of their clauses. Legal reglementation is substituted for contractual reglementation. The contract is no more than the submission of the parties to an obligatory regime."

Things have not gone so far in the English-speaking world. But they are moving in the same direction. We have been developing much "contractual dirigism." Standard contracts, statutory obligatory clauses in contracts, statutory and administrative prescribing of contract provisions, and administrative control over making, performing, and enforcing of contracts are becoming everyday matters.

Friedmann, looking at the matter from a functional standpoint, considers that state prescribing rather than mere state enforcing of contracts is called for by the bigness of things in the economy of today, which precludes the equality of the parties that the regime of free contract presupposed and throws us back upon the service state to insure the fulfillment of reasonable expectations which are increasingly beyond the reach of the ordinary man.

As to the moral or humanitarian idea in the disappearance of free contract, what the French writers have noted has been going on gradually also in American law and has been gaining impetus for a generation. There is a notable tendency in recent writing everywhere to insist, not as did the nineteenth century that the debtor keep faith in all cases even though it ruin him and his family, but that the creditor must take a risk also, either along with or in some cases instead of the debtor.

Limitations on the power of a creditor to exact satisfaction from a debtor's property have a long history. In the classical period of Roman law as between certain debtors and certain creditors there was a benefit or privilege of being held only for what the debtor could pay without being deprived of the means of subsistence. In certain relations it was deemed impious for one to strip the other of everything he had and leave him a pauper. This doctrine was rejected by French law in the nineteenth century. But recent codes and legislation in continental Europe have provided a number of restrictions upon the power of the creditor to exact satisfaction. These were at first likened to the Roman privilege but were based on ideas of social justice rather than of religion. They are now referred to a general public service of relieving debtors as a function of the state in order to promote the general welfare by releasing men from the burden of poverty. Laws exempting the family home, at least up to a certain value, from seizure or execution, and exempting furniture, implements of husbandry, tools, the library of a practicing member of a profession, and the wages of a worker, began to be enacted in the United States more than one hundred years ago, and such exemption laws have been greatly extended in the present century. Chiefly they have been designed to protect the family and dependents of the debtor, but partly to secure the social interest in the individual life. Today, however, there is a changed spirit behind these exemptions. There is a spirit of recognizing a claim upon society to relieve men of burdens they have freely and fairly assumed, on the assumption that thus relieving them is a service to the whole community which the state has been set up to perform. A debtor is by no means always the under-

dog which humanitarian thinking postulates. The creditor
may be a guardian of orphans or a trustee for a widow and
the debtor a well-to-do speculator who has taken on too
much and seeks to shake off an inconvenient load. "Favor
to debtors," as the French call their policy of today, may
in particular cases put the balance of hardship upon creditors
who on humanitarian principles make the more meritorious
appeal.

How far the humanitarian doctrine of favor to debtors
may take us is illustrated by a theory of contract now taught
by some teachers of law. They put forth what they call the
prediction theory of contract. A contract is a prediction
of ability and willingness to do something at some time
in the future. The bonds and notes of municipalities, public
utilities, and industrial corporations under recent legislation
as to reorganization come to something very like this.

Legislation impairing or doing away with the practical
legal means of enforcing promises is now upheld on the basis
of a doctrine that the power of the legislature to relieve promisors of liability is implied in the sovereignty of the state.
Such relief is one of the services the state is set up to render.
It is significant to note how this has been made to comport
with a limitation upon state legislation prescribed in the Constitution of the United States.

After resumption of grants and revocation of franchises
at turns of political fortune in seventeenth-century England,
and of colonial legislation and state legislation in the depres-
sion after the Revolution interfering with enforcement of
contracts and revoking charters, the Federal Constitution
prohibited state legislation impairing the obligation of contracts. But that provision of the Constitution has now, for
the larger part at least, become a mere preachment, and the
spirit that has led to substitution of a mere preachment for
an enforceable constitutional provision has been affecting

regard for the upholding of promises on every side. There is no longer a strong feeling of moral duty to perform. When to the lack of this feeling is added impairment of the legal duty as well, it undermines a main pillar of the economic order.

Again bankruptcy relief and discharge or adjustment of indebtedness have been extended in recent years so as to make escape from debts as easy as incurring them. For a generation legislation has increasingly limited the power of the creditor to collect, has created more and larger exemptions, and has added much to the once narrowly limited number who may escape through bankruptcy. This has been rested avowedly on the powers of the service state. Statutes allowing municipalities to "reorganize" their debts are upheld, so the courts tell us, by "extending the police power into economic welfare." Undoubtedly the quest of certainty, uniformity, and stability in the nineteenth century carried what might be called a hard-boiled attitude toward debtors too far. But that attitude had succeeded an era of individualized justice and overreliance upon the personal feelings of the judge. It should be possible to avoid an extreme of counter-reaction in zeal to be humane today. In an extreme of humanitarian thinking we may lose sight of the social interest in the security of transactions and of the threat to the economic order which is involved.

If letting people of full age and sound mind contract freely and holding them rigidly to the contracts they made was carried to an extreme in the last century, a system of restricting free contract and relaxing the obligation of contract may be carried quite as far in reaction, and the spirit of the time seems to be pushing everywhere to that other extreme. The man of high moral sense, who after bankruptcy in time voluntarily paid off his barred debts used to be pointed out as an example of the just and upright man to whom his neighbors looked up. Today I fear he would be set down a fool.

But the movement to relieve promisors is not confined to legislation. Anglo-American courts have been doing their share in building up a body of doctrine as to frustration. A law teacher now tells us that there is "a real need for a field in human intercourse freed from legal restraint, for a field where men may without liability withdraw assurances they have once given." The one-time general proposition that courts cannot make contracts over for the parties, that freedom of contract implies the possibility of contracting foolishly, is giving way to a power of the service state to act as guardian of persons of age, sound mind, and discretion, and relieve them by judicial action from their contracts, or make their contracts over for them, or make their promises easier for them. We are now told that even where a contract contains provisions as to the consequences of particular possible frustration the courts may recognize other frustrations and apply other consequences to them. Often the words finally written in a contract after a long negotiation are the result of hard-fought compromises. They are not ideal provisions from the standpoint of either side, but are what each is willing to concede in order to reach agreement. After some frustrating event has happened and a party who has suffered damage from nonperformance is suing for it, to say that he intended and would have consented to insert a condition which the court conjures up to relieve the promisor is to make a new contract under a fiction of interpretation. This sort of interpretation, which has much vogue in the service state, is said by a judge of one of our courts to be a process of distillation. We are told that the meaning is distilled from the words. It might be suggested that distilling is often illicit and the product moonshine.

So much in everyday life depends upon reliance on promises that an everyday dependence loses its effectiveness if

promises are to be performed only when it suits the promisor's convenience. A promise which imposes no risk on the
promisor belongs to the prediction theory. It is not a promise.
A promisee reasonably expects a promise to be performed
even if it hurts. Why relieve only the promisor? Is not the
promisee frustrated if he cannot have what was promised
him?

Forty years ago sociologists were saying that social control
through law having put down force in the relations of men
with each other must now take the next step and put down
cunning. But all depends on what is meant by cunning. Are
we to say that superior knowledge, diligence, ability to fore-
see, and judgment as to persons and things are to be allowed
to have no influence in transactions? Undoubtedly men desire to be equal in all respects. But they also desire to be free.
They desire to be allowed to use the qualities and capacities
with which they have been born. Carrying out satisfaction
of the desire to be equal to its fullest development would
reduce all activity to the lowest possible attainment. No one
would be allowed to exert himself beyond the capacity of
the least efficient. Men's desire to be equal and their desire
to be free must be kept in balance. Either carried to the extreme negates the other.

In truth in government, as in all else that men do, balance
is called for. He that believeth, says Isaiah, shall not make
haste. Ultimate perfection of mankind, if we may trust experience, can no more be achieved through government than
through the other universal agencies of perfection in which
men have believed in the past. Additional services by the state,
where they can be performed by the state without waste of
what we have learned to do well by other institutions without reducing the individual man to passive obedience or to
parasitism, is a reasonable program which need not carry us
to the omnicompetent state.

Bibliography

GENERAL

Recent Expositions and General Theories

My Philosophy of Law, Credos of Sixteen American Scholars, 1941. Published under direction of Julius Rosenthal Foundation, Northwestern University.

Stone, The Province and Function of Law, 1946.

Friedmann, Legal Theory, 1944, 2d ed. 1949.

Interpretations of Modern Legal Philosophies, ed. by Paul Sayre, 1947.

Cairns, Legal Philosophy from Plato to Hegel 1949.

Cohen and Cohen, Readings in Jurisprudence and Legal Philosophy, 1951.

Berolzheimer, The World's Legal Philosophies, trans. by Jastrow, 1912.

CHAPTER I

1. *In Antiquity*

Plato (B.C. 427–347), Republic, Laws. Translations in Jowett's Plato. The translation of the Republic is published separately.

Pseudo-Plato, Minos. Now generally considered not to be a genuine work of Plato and variously dated from as early as *c*. 337 B.C. to as late as *c*. 250 B.C. There is a convenient translation in Bohn's Libraries.

Aristotle (B.C. 384–322), Nicomachean Ethics. Convenient trans-
lation in McKeon, Basic Works of Aristotle (1941).
——— Politics. Translation by Jowett should be used.
Cicero (B.C. 106–43), De Legibus. Convenient translation by
Keyes in the Loeb Classical Series.

2. The Scholastic Theological Jurists
Thomas Aquinas (1225–74), Summa Theologiae, edited by
Migne, 1877. Rickaby, Aquinas Ethicus (1896), is a convenient
translation of the portions relating to law.

3. The Protestant Jurist Theologians
Oldendorp, Iuris naturalis gentium et civilis εἰσαγώγη, 1539.
Hemmingius (Hemmingsen), De iure naturale apodictica meth-
odus, 1562.
Winckler, Principiorum iuris libri V 1615.

*These are collected conveniently in Kaltenborn, Die Vorläufer
des Hugo Grotius.*

4. The Spanish Jurist Theologians
Soto, De iustitia et iure (1589).
Suarez, De legibus ac deo legislatore (1619).

*Reference may be made to Figgis, Studies of Political Thought
from Gerson to Grotius, lect. 5.*

5. The Law of Nature School
Grotius, De iure belli ac pacis (1625). Whewell's edition with
an abridged translation is convenient.
Pufendorf, De iure naturae et gentium (1672). Kennet's transla-
tion (1703) may be found in many editions.
Burlamaqui, Principes du droit naturel (1747). Nugent's transla-
tion is convenient.
Wolff, Institutiones iuris naturae et gentium, 1750.
Rutherforth, Institutes of Natural Law, 1754–56.
Vattel, Le Droit des gens, Préliminaires, 1758. There are many
translations.
Rousseau, Le Contrat social, 1762. Tozer's translation is con-
venient.

Blackstone, Commentaries on the Laws of England, *1* (1765), § 2, 38–62.

6. *The Forerunners of Analytical Jurisprudence*

Hobbes, Leviathan, 1651. This may be found in Molesworth's edition of Hobbes' *English Works*, but has often been reprinted separately.

Spinoza, Ethica, 1674. The translation by Gutmann (1949) can be recommended.

―――― Tractatus theologico-politicus, 1670. The translation by Elwes in Bohn's Libraries must be used with caution.

7. *The English Utilitarians*

Bentham, Principles of Morals and Legislation, 1780. A convenient reprint (1879) was published by the Clarendon Press.

―――― Theory of Legislation (originally published in French, 1820). Hildreth's translation (1864) has gone through many editions.

Mill, On Liberty, 1859. Courtney's edition (1892) is convenient.

On the English Utilitarians see Dicey, Lectures on the Relation between Law and Public Opinion in England, 2d ed. 1914, lect. 6; Albee, History of English Utilitarianism, 1902; Stephen, The English Utilitarians, 1900.

8. *The Metaphysical School*

Kant, Metaphysische Anfangsgründe der Rechtslehre, 2d ed. 1798. Translated by Hastie as Kant's Philosophy of Law, 1887.

Fichte, Grundlage des Naturrechts; 1796; new ed. by Medicus, 1908. Translated by Kroeger as The Science of Rights (1889).

Hegel, Grundlinien der Philosophie des Rechts, 1821; ed. by Gans, 1840; new ed. by Lasson, 1911. Translated by Knox, 1942. The translation by Dyde as Hegel's Philosophy of Right (1896) is not good.

Krause, Abriss des Systemes der Philosophie des Rechtes, 1828.

Ahrens, Cours de droit naturel, 1837, 8th ed. 1892. Twenty-four editions in seven languages. The German 6th edition (Naturrecht, 1870–71) contains important matter not in the French editions.

Green, Principles of Political Obligation, 1911. Lectures delivered in 1879–80, reprinted from Green's Complete Works.
Lorimer, Institutes of Law, 2d ed. 1880.
Lasson, Lehrbuch der Rechtsphilosophie, 1882.
Miller, Lectures on the Philosophy of Law, 1884.
Boistel, Cours de philosophie du droit, 1870; new ed. 1899.
Brown, The Underlying Principles of Modern Legislation, 1912.

On the metaphysical school see Gray, Nature and Sources of the Law (1st ed. 1909), §§ 7–9; Bryce, Studies in History and Jurisprudence, Essay 12; Pollock, Essays in Jurisprudence and Ethics, 1–30; Korkunov, General Theory of Law, trans. by Hastings, § 4; Bergbohm, Jurisprudenz und Rechtsphilosophie, §§ 6–15; Pound, The Scope and Purpose of Sociological Jurisprudence, 24 Harvard Law Rev. 691, 604–611.

9. The Social Philosophical Schools

The Social Utilitarians

Jhering, Der Zweck im Recht, 1877–83, 6th–8th ed. 1923. The first volume is translated by Husik under the title Law as a Means to an End, 1913.

———— Scherz und Ernst in der Jurisprudenz, 1884; 9th ed. 1904.

Some significant extracts are translated in Vinogradoff, Historical Jurisprudence 1 (1920), 25–26. On the social Utilitarians see the appendices to Jhering, Law as a Means to an End, trans. by Husik; Berolzheimer, The World's Legal Philosophies, trans. by Jastrow, 327–351; Korkunov, General Theory of Law, trans. by Hastings, §§ 13–17; Pound, The Scope and Purpose of Sociological Jurisprudence, 25 Harvard Law Rev. 140, 140–147 (1911); idem, Fifty Years of Jurisprudence, 51 Harvard Law Rev. 444, 447 (1938).

The Neo-Kantians

Stammler, Wirtschaft und Recht, 1896; 5th ed. 1924.

———— Lehre von dem rechtigen Rechte, 1902; new ed. 1926. The first edition is translated by Husik as the Theory of Justice, 1925.

———— Die Gesetzmässigkeit in Rechtsordnung und Volkswirtschaft, 1902.

———— Systematische Theorie der Rechtswissenschaft, 1911.

———— Rechts- und Staatstheorien der Neuzeit, 1917.

———— Rechtsphilosophische Abhandlungen, 1925.

The most significant paper here is Über die Methode der geschichtlichen Rechtstheorie (1888) in 1, 1.

Del Vecchio, The Formal Bases of Law, trans. by Lisle, 1914. A translation of I presupposti filosofici della nozione del diritto, 1905; Il concetto del diritto, 1906, reprinted 1912; Il concetto della natura e il principio del diritto, 1908.

———— Lezioni di filosofia del diritto, 1930; 3d ed. 1936. French translation as Leçons de philosophie du droit (1936) by Le Fur.

———— Justice, An Historical and Philosophical Essay, translated and edited with additional notes by Campbell, 1952.

See Vinogradoff, Common Sense in Law (1914), chap. 9; Kaufmann, Kritik der neukantischen Rechtsphilosophie (1926); Pound, The Scope and Purpose of Sociological Jurisprudence, 25 Harvard Law Rev. 140, 147–154 (1911); idem, Fifty Years of Jurisprudence, 51 Harvard Law Rev. 444, 448–452 (1938); Friedmann, Legal Theory (2d ed. 1949), 87 ff.

The Neo-Hegelians

Kohler, Rechtsphilosophie und Universalrechtsgeschichte, in Holtzendorff, Enzyklopädie der Rechtswissenschaft (6th ed. 1904; 7th ed. 1913), Vol. 1. Not in prior editions.

———— Lehrbuch der Rechtsphilosophie, 1909; 2d ed. 1917. Translated by Albrecht as Philosophy of Law, 1914.

———— Moderne Rechtsprobleme, 1907; 2d ed. 1913.

Berolzheimer, System der Rechts- und Wirtschaftsphilosophie, Vol. 3 (1906), general system of legal and economic philosophy.

See Pound, Interpretations of Legal History (1923), 141–151; idem, The Scope and Purpose of Sociological Jurisprudence, 25 Harvard Law Rev. 154–158 (1911); idem, Fifty Years of Jurisprudence, 51 Harvard Law Rev. 444, 452–453 (1938).

The Neo-idealists

Tourtoulon, Principes philosophiques de l'histoire du droit, 1908–
19. Translated by Read as Philosophy in the Development of
Law, 1922, Neo-Kantian psychological-logical.

Radbruch, Rechtsphilosophie, 3d ed. 1932; 4th ed. 1950. Spanish
translation by Echavarría as Filosofia del derecho, 1933. First
ed. as Grundzüge der Rechtsphilosophie, 1914, trans. by Wilk
in 20th-Century Legal Philosophy Series, *4* (1950), 47–224.
Neo-Kantian antinomic. For exposition and critique of Radbruch, see Gurvitch, Une philosophie antinomique du droit—
Gustav Radbruch, Archives de philosophie du droit et de sociologie juridique (1932), 530; Pound, Fifty Years of Jurisprudence, 51 Harvard Law Rev. 444, 454–460 (1938).

——— Einführung in die Rechtswissenschaft, 9th ed. 1929.

——— Vorschule der Rechtsphilosophie, 1947.

Huber, Recht und Rechtsverwirklichung, 1921; 2d ed. 1925.

Hocking, The Present Status of the Philosophy of Law and of
Rights, 1926.

Lask, Rechtsphilosophie, 1905, in Gesammelte Schriften (1923),
1, 278–331. Translated by Wilk in 20th-Century Legal Philosophy Series, *4* (1950), 3–42.

Binder, Philosophie des Rechts, 1925. "An idealistic philosophy as
a system of ideal propositions which find their fulfilment in
the empirical world of the law, and according to which, therefore, we judge the structure of this law."

Recaséns Siches, Vida humana sociedad y derecho, 1939.

10. *Juristic Phenomenology*

*See Schapp, Die neue Wissenschaft vom Recht, 1931–32; Schreier,
Grundbegriffe und Grundformen des Rechts, 1924, Spanish trans.
as Concepto y formas fundamentales del derecho, 1942 with Introduction by L. Recaséns Siches; G. Husserl, Recht und Welt,
1930; idem, Rechtskraft und Rechtsgeltung, 1925; idem, Der
Rechtsgegenstand, 1933.*

11. *Revived Natural Law*

Fuller, The Law in Quest of Itself, 1940.

M. R. Cohen, Reason and Nature, in Cohen and Cohen, Readings in Jurisprudence and Legal Philosophy (1951), 615–635.

See also Modern French Legal Philosophy in Modern Legal Philosophy Series, Vol. 7 (1916).

Neo-metaphysical

Demogue, Les Notions fondamentales du droit privé (1911). Trans. in Modern French Legal Philosophy, Modern Legal Philosophy Series, 7 (1916), 347–372.

Sauter, Die philosophischen Grundlagen des Naturrechts, 1932.

Neo-Scholastic

Gény, Méthode d'interprétation et sources en droit privé positif, 1899; 2d ed. 1919. A book of the first importance. Parts of the first edition are translated in Science of Legal Method, Modern Legal Philosophy Series, 9 (1917), 1–46. See Wortley, François Gény, in Modern Theories of Law, 139–159.

———, Science et technique en droit privé postif, Vol. 1 (1913), Vol. 2 (1915), Vol. 3 (1921), Vol. 4 (1924).

On Gény, see Pound, Fifty Years of Jurisprudence, 51 Harvard Law Rev. 444, 464–466 (1938); Jones, Modern Discussions of the Aims and Methods of Legal Science, 47 Law Quarterly Rev. 62, 67–73; Gurvitch, L'Idée du droit social (1932), 216–227.

Dabin, La Philosophie de l'ordre juridique positif, 1929. Trans. by Wilk in The Legal Philosophies of Lask, Radbruch and Dabin, in 20th-Century Legal Philosophy Series, 4 (1950), 227–470.

Réglado, Valeur sociale et concept juridiques, norme et technique, 1950. See Horváth, Social Value and Reality in Current French Legal Thought, 1 Am. Jour. of Comparative Law 243 (1952).

Positive Sociological

Duguit, L'état, le droit objectif, et la loi positive (1901). Chaps. 8–11 are translated in Modern French Legal Philosophy, Modern Legal Philosophy Series, 7 (1916), 237–344.

Duguit, L'état, le droit social, le droit individuel et la transforma-
tion de l'état, 3d ed. 1922.

——— Les Transformations générales du droit privé, 1912. Translated in Progress of Continental Law in the Nineteenth Century, Continental Legal History Series, Vol. *11* (1918), chap. 3.

——— Les Transformations du droit public, 1913. Trans. by
Laski as Law in the Modern State.

——— Law and the State, trans. by De Sloovère, 31 Harvard Law
Rev. 1 (1917).

——— Leçons de droit public général, 1926.

> For appreciations and critiques of Duguit, see Pound, Fifty
> Years of Jurisprudence, 51 Harvard Law Rev. 444, 466–
> 471; Bonnard, Léon Duguit, 3 Revue internationale de la
> théorie du droit, 58–70; Gurvitch, Sociology of Law, 132–
> 134.

12. The Economic Interpretation

Dicey, Lectures on the Relation between Law and Public Opinion in England in the Nineteenth Century, 1905; 2d ed. 1914.
Note especially the preface.

Centralization and Law (1906), with an Introduction by M. M.
Bigelow. Five lectures at Boston University Law School: 1,
Nature of Law, by Brooks Adams, and 2, Law under Inequal-
ity: Monopoly, by Brooks Adams, are of chief importance.

Adams, The Modern Conception of Animus, 19 Green Bag 12
(1907).

Leist, Privatrecht und Kapitalismus im neunzehnten Jahrhundert,
1911.

Croce, Riduzione della filosofia del diritto alla filosofia dell'
economia, 1907.

*See Pound, Interpretations of Legal History (1923), lect. 5; idem,
The Economic Interpretation and the Law of Torts, 53 Harvard
Law Rev. 365.*

13. Juristic Socialist

Menger, Das bürgerliche Recht und die besitzlosen Volksklassen,
1889; 5th ed. 1927.

———— Über die sozialen Aufgaben des Rechts, 1895; 3d ed. 1910.

Picard, Le Droit pur, 1899; reprinted 1920.

Panunzio, Il socialismo giuridico, 2d ed. 1911.

Barasch, Le Socialisme juridique, 1923. Contains a full bibliography.

Lévy, Les Fondements de droit, 1933. For a critique, see Gurvitch, Expérience juridique et la philosophie pluraliste du droit, 170–200; *idem*, Sociology of Law, 134–139.

Paschukanis, The General Theory of Law and Marxism, in Soviet Legal Philosophy, 20th-Century Legal Philosophy Series, 5 (1951), 111–225. There is a German translation, Allgemeine Rechtslehre und Marxismus (1929), from the Russian 3d ed. 1927. See Pound, Fifty Years of Jurisprudence, 51 Harvard Law Rev. 777, 779–782 (1938); Dobrin, Soviet Jurisprudence and Socialism, 52 Law Quarterly Rev. 402 (1936); Gsovski, The Soviet Concept of Law, 7 Fordham Law Rev. 1 (1938).

14. *The Neo-realists*

Lundstedt, Superstition or Rationality in Action for Peace, 1925.

———— Die Unwissenschaftlichkeit der Rechtswissenschaft, 1932–36.

Frank, Law and the Modern Mind, 1931.

Arnold, The Symbols of Government, 1935.

Robinson, Law and the Lawyers, 1935.

Garlan, Legal Realism and Justice, 1941.

Seagle, The Quest for Law, 1941. Historical-realist, critical of philosophical jurisprudence and of skeptical realism.

See Cardozo, Address before New York State Bar Association, 55 Rep. New York State Bar Assn. 263, 267–307 (1932); Pound, Fifty Years of Jurisprudence, 51 Harvard Law Rev. 777, 779–799 (1938); idem, The Call for a Realist Jurisprudence, 44 Harvard Law Rev. 697 (1931); Llewellyn, Some Realism about Realism, 44 Harvard Law Rev. 1222 (1931); Fuller, American Legal Realism, 82 University of Pennsylvania Law Rev. 429 (1934); Kantorowicz, Some Rationalism about Realism, 43 Yale Law Jour. 1240 (1934); Llewellyn, A Realistic Jurisprudence—the Next Step, 30 Columbia Law Rev. 431 (1930); Pound, Contemporary

Juristic Theory (*1940*), lect. *2; Fuller, The Law in Quest of It-self* (*1940*), *52–65; Goodhart, Some American Interpretations of Law, in Modern Legal Theories* (*1933*), *1–20.*

15. Sociological

Mechanical and Positivist

Spencer, Justice, 1891.

Rueff, Des sciences physiques aux sciences morales, 1922. Trans. by Green as From the Physical to the Social Sciences, 1929.

Biological and Ethnological

Post, Der Ursprung des Rechts, 1876.

—— Die Grundlagen des Rechts und die Grundzüge seiner Entwickelungsgeschichte, 1884.

—— Grundriss der ethnologischen Jurisprudenz, 1894–95.

Kuhlenbeck, Natürliche Grundlagen des Rechts, 1905. A discussion of fundamental problems of jurisprudence from the Darwinian standpoint.

Richard, L'Origine de l'idée de droit, 1892.

Vaccaro, Les Bases sociologiques du droit et de l'état, 1898. A translation of Le basi del diritto e dello stato. A theory of law as the outcome of class struggles.

See Pound, Interpretations of Legal History (*1923*), *69–91.*

Psychological

Tarde, Les Transformations du droit, 1894; 6th ed. 1909.

Vanni, Lezioni di filosofia del diritto, 1901–2; 4th ed. 1920.

Psychological Intuitionist

Petrazycki, Methodologie der Theorien des Rechts und der Moral, 1933, in Opera Academiae Universalis Jurisprudentiae Comparativae, Series 2, Studia, fasc. 2.

—— Über die Motive des Handelns und über das Wesen der Moral und des Rechts; trans. from the Russian by Balson, 1907.

See Modern Legal Theories (*1933*), *21–37.*

Experimental Positivist

Vacca, Il diritto sperimentale (1923).

See Wigmore, Problems of Law (1920), 48–61; Beutel, Some Implications of Experimental Jurisprudence, 41 Harvard Law Rev. 169 (1934); idem, An Outline of the Nature and Methods of Experimental Jurisprudence, 51 Columbia Law Rev. 415 (1951).

The Stage of Unification

On this stage in sociology see Durkheim, Les Règles de la méthode sociologique, 6th ed. 1912.

Holmes, The Path of the Law, 10 Harvard Law Rev. 467 (1897), reprinted in Holmes, Collected Papers, 167–202.

—— Law in Science and Science in Law, 12 Harvard Law Rev. 443 (1899) reprinted in Holmes, Collected Papers, 210–243.

Wurzel, Das juristische Denken, 98–102 (1904). Translated in Modern Legal Philosophy Series, 9 (1917), 421–428.

Gnaeus Flavius (Kantorowicz), Der Kampf um die Rechtswissenschaft, 1906.

Kornfeld, Soziale Machtverhältnisse: Grundzüge einer allgemeinen Lehre vom positiven Rechte auf soziologischer Grundlage, 1911.

Ehrlich, Erforschung des lebenden Rechts in 35 Schmollers Jahrbuch für Gesetzgebung 129 (1911).

—— Grundlegung der Soziologie des Rechts, 1913; 2d ed. 1929. Translated by Moll as Fundamental Principles of the Sociology of Law, 1936.

See critique by Vinogradoff, The Crisis of Modern Jurisprudence, 29 Yale Law Jour. 312; and reviews of the English version by Simpson, 51 Harvard Law Rev. 190; by Timasheff, 2 Am. Sociological Rev. 120; and by Rheinstein, 48 Internat. Jour. of Ethics, 232. Also critique by Gurvitch, Sociology of Law, 148–156; appreciation by Pound, Fifty Years of Jurisprudence, 51 Harvard Law Rev. 777, 805–806 (1938).

—— Das lebende Recht der Völker von Bukowina, 1913.

—— Die juristische Logik, 1918.

Page, Professor Ehrlich's Czernowitz Seminar of Living Law,

Proc. 14th Annual Meeting of Assn. of Am. Law Schools
(1914), 46.

Kornfeld, Allgemeine Rechtslehre und Jurisprudenz, 1920.

Cardozo, The Nature of the Judicial Process, 1921.

────── The Growth of the Law, 1924.

────── Paradoxes of Legal Science, 1928.

Pontes Miranda, Systema de sciencia positiva do direito, 1932.

Jerusalem, Soziologie des Rechts, Gesetzmässigkeit und Kollek-
tivität, 1925.

Burckhardt, Methode und System des Rechts, 1936.

Sauer, Rechts und Staatsphilosophie, 1936.

Bodenheimer, Jurisprudence, 1940.

Cairns, The Theory of Legal Science, 1941. Behaviorist sociological.

The Methodological Stage: Sociology of Law

Weber, Rechtssoziologie in Wirtschaft und Gesellschaft (1st
ed. 1922; 2d ed. in 2 vols. 1925), Part 2, chap. 2.

Horváth, Rechtssoziologie, 1934. See review by Wilson (1936)
52 Law Quarterly Rev. 138; Pound, Fifty Years of Jurisprudence, 51 Harvard Law Rev. 777, 806–807 (1938).

Timasheff, Introduction to the Sociology of Law, 1939.

Sauer, Juristische Methodenlehre, 1940.

Gurvitch, Sociology of Law, 1942. Supersedes the author's Élé-
ments de sociologie du droit, 1939.

Llewellyn and Hoebel, The Cheyenne Way: Conflict and Case
Law in Primitive Jurisprudence, 1941.

*See also Llewellyn, On Reading and Using the New Jurispru-
dence, 40 Columbia Law Rev. 581 (1940); idem, The Normative,
the Legal, and the Law Jobs: The Problem of Juristic Method,
49 Yale Law Jour. 1355 (1940). See appreciation by Gurvitch,
Sociology of Law, 178–183.*

Neo-scholastic Sociological Jurisprudence

Hauriou, La Théorie de l'institution et de la fondation, in La
Cité moderne et les transformations du droit, 1925.

Renard, La Théorie de l'institution, 1930.

See the papers in Archives de philosophie du droit et de sociologie juridique (1931), especially Delos, La Théorie de l'institution, 97–153, and Gurvitch, Les Idée-maîtresses de Maurice Hauriou. Also Gurvitch, Sociology of Law, 139–147; Pound, Fifty Years of Jurisprudence, 51 Harvard Law Rev. 777, 807–809 (1938); Jennings, The Institutional Theory, in Modern Theories of Law (1933), 68–85. Reference may be made also to recent Spanish writings noted in Recaséns Siches, Estudios de filosofía del derecho (1936), 489–492.

CHAPTER 2

Pound, The End of Law as Developed in Legal Rules and Doctrines, 27 Harvard Law Rev. 195 (1913).

—— The End of Law as Developed in Juristic Thought, 27 Harvard Law Rev. 605 (1914), 30 Harvard Law Rev. 201 (1917).

—— Twentieth Century Ideas as to the End of Law, in Harvard Legal Essays (1934), 357–375.

—— Liberty of Contract, 18 Yale Law Jour. 454 (1909).

Berolzheimer, The World's Legal Philosophies trans. by Jastrow (1912), §§ 17–29, 35–37, 43–48, 52.

Stone, The Province and Function of Law (1946), pt. 2, Introductory Note and chaps. 8–16.

Friedmann, Legal Theory (2d ed. 1949), chap. 19.

Demogue, Les Notions fondamentales du droit privé (1911), 63–110, 119–142.

Figgis, Studies of Political Thought from Gerson to Grotius (1907), lect. 6.

Korkunov, General Theory of Law, trans. by Hastings (1909), 55–64, 320–322.

Charmont, La Renaissance de droit naturel (1910), 10–43.

Hobbes, Leviathan (1651), chap. 15. Use the text in Molesworth's edition of Hobbes' English Works, Vol. 1.

Kant, Metaphysische Anfangsgründe der Rechtslehre, 2d ed. 1798. Trans. in part by Hastie as Kant's Philosophy of Law, 1887.

Spencer, Justice (1891), chaps. 5, 6.

Maine, Early History of Institutions 1874; American ed., 398–400.

Stephen, Liberty, Equality, Fraternity (1873), 189–255.

Mill, On Liberty (1859), chap. 4.

Jhering, Scherz und Ernst in die Jurisprudenz (1884, 13th ed. 1924), pt. 3.

Miller, The Data of Jurisprudence (1903), chap. 6.

Salmond, Jurisprudence (1902; 10th ed. 1947), § 9.

Bentham, Theory of Legislation, Principles of the Civil Code. Trans. by Hildreth, 1864; 5th ed. 1887; new ed. by Ogden, 1931. Pt. 1, chaps. 1–7.

Holland, Elements of Jurisprudence (1880; 13th ed. 1924), chap. 6.

Picard, Le Droit pur (1899), liv. 9.

Holmes, Common Law (1881), lect. 1.

Fehr, Hammurapi und das Salische Recht (1910), 135–138.

Seagle, The Quest for Law (1941), 27–149.

Ames, Law and Morals, 22 Harvard Law Rev. 97 (1908).

Gray, Nature and Sources of the Law (1st ed. 1909), § 58. Somewhat different in 2d edition (1921).

Dicey, Law and Public Opinion in England (1905), lect. 6.

Stammler, Wesen des Rechts und der Rechtswissenschaft, in Systematische Theorie der Rechtswissenschaft (1911), i–lix.

Kohler, Rechtsphilosophie und Universalrechtsgeschichte, in Enzyklopädie der Rechtswissenschaft (1904; new ed. 1913), Vol. 1, §§ 13–16, 33–34, 51.

CHAPTER 3

Stone, The Province and Function of Law (1946), 137–206.

Gény, Méthode d'interprétation et sources en droit privé positif, 2d ed. 1919.

Cardozo, The Nature of the Judicial Process, 1921.

—— The Growth of the Law, 1924.

—— Paradoxes of Legal Science, 1928.

Vander Eycken, Méthode positive de l'interprétation juridique, 1907.

Mallieux, L'Exégèse des codes, 1908.

Ransson, Essai sur l'art de juger, 1912. See Wigmore, Problems of Law, 65–101; Pound, the Enforcement of Law, 20 Green Bag 401; *idem*, Courts and Legislation, 7 Am. Political Science Rev. 361–383.

Science of Legal Method, Modern Legal Philosophy Series, Vol. 9 (1917).

Gnaeus Flavius (Kantorowicz), Der Kampf um die Rechtswissenschaft, 1906.

Fuchs, Recht und Wahrheit in unserer heutigen Justiz, 1908.

—— Die Gemeinschädlichkeit der konstruktiven Jurisprudenz, 1909.

Oertmann, Gesetzeszwang und Richterfreiheit, 1909.

Rumpf, Gesetz und Richter, 1906.

Brütt, Die Kunst der Rechtsanwendung, 1907.

Gmelin, Quousque? Beiträge zur soziologischen Rechtsfindung, 1910.

Reichel, Gesetz und Richterspruch, 1915.

Jellinek, Gesetz, Gesetzesanwendung und Zweckmässigkeitserwägung, 1913.

Kübl, Das Rechtsgefühl, 1913.

Heck, Gesetzesauslegung und Interessenjurisprudenz, 1914.

Stampe, Grundriss der Wertbewegungslehre, 1912, 1919.

Pound, Theory of Judicial Decision, 36 Harvard Law Rev. 641, 802, 940 (1923).

Cairns, Legal Philosophy from Plato to Hegel (1949), 236–241.

Frank, Courts on Trial (1949), chaps. 21, 23.

Cohen and Cohen, Readings in Jurisprudence and Legal Philosophy (1951), chap. 6.

See Kohler, Lehrbuch des bürgerlichen Rechts, Vol. 1, §§ 38–40; Austin Jurisprudence, Essay on Interpretation (5th ed.), 989–1001 (1885); Pound, Spurious Interpretation, 7 Columbia Law Rev. 379; Gray, Nature and Sources of the Law (1 ed. 1909), §§ 370–399; Somlo, Juristische Grundlehre, §§ 110–122; Stammler, Rechts- und Staatstheorien der Neuzeit, § 18; Pound, Introduction to English trans. of Saleilles' Individualization of Punishment; Saleilles,

*Individualization of Punishment, trans. by Jastrow, chap. 9;
Pound, Administrative Applications of Legal Standards, 44 Rep.
Am. Bar Assn., 445; Laun, Das freie Ermessen und seine Grenzen,
1910.*

CHAPTER 4

Holmes, Collected Papers (1920), 49–116.
Baty, Vicarious Liability, 1916.
Hasse, Die Culpa des römischen Rechts, 2d ed. 1838.
Jhering, Der Schuldmoment im römischen Privatrecht, 1867.
Rümelin, Schadensersatz ohne Verschulden, 1910.
Triandafil, L'Idée de faute et l'idée de risque comme fondement
　　de la responsabilité, 1914.
Pound, New Paths of the Law (1950), lect. 2.
Lundstedt, General Principles of Civil Liability, Acta Academiae
　　Universalis Jurisprudentiae Comparativae, 2, pt. 2 (1934), 367.
Friedmann, Law and Social Change in Contemporary Britain
　　(1951), 73–101.

*See Binding, Die Normen und ihre Übertretung, Vol. 1, §§ 50–51;
Meumann, Prolegomena zu einem System des Vermögensrechts
(1903), 80 ff.; Duguit in Progress of Continental Law in the
Nineteenth Century, Continental Legal History Series, 11 (1918),
124–128; Gény, Risque et responsabilité, 1 Revue trimestrielle de
droit civil, 812; Rolin, Responsabilité sans faute, 38 Revue de
droit international et législation comparée, 64; Demogue, Fault,
Risk and Apportionment of Risk of Responsibility, 15 Illinois
Law Rev. 369; Thayer, Liability without Fault, 29 Harvard Law
Rev. 801; Smith, Tort and Absolute Liability, 30 Harvard Law
Rev. 241, 319, 409; Bohlen, The Rule in Rylands v. Fletcher, 59
University of Pennsylvania Law Rev. 298, 373, 423; Isaacs, Fault
and Liability, 31 Harvard Law Rev. 954.*

CHAPTER 5

Ely, Property and Contract in Their Relation to the Distribution
　　of Wealth (1914), 1, 51–93, 132–258, 295–443; 2, 475–549.

Hobhouse and Others, Property, Its Duties and Rights, Historically, Philosophically and Religiously Regarded (2d ed. 1915), essays, 1–3, 5–8.

Noyes, The Institution of Property, 1936.

Renner, The Institutions of Private Law and Their Social Functions, ed. by Kahn-Freund, 1949.

Friedmann, Law and Social Change in Contemporary Britain, (1951), chap. 2.

Green, Principles of Political Obligation (1911), §§ 211–231.

Miller, Lectures on the Philosophy of Law (1884), lect. 5.

Herkless, Jurisprudence (1901), chap. 10.

Russell, Principles of Social Reconstruction (1916), chap. 4.

Spencer, Justice (1891), chap. 12.

Kohler, Philosophy of Law, trans. by Albrecht (1914), 120–133.

Maine, Ancient Law (1861; new ed. by Sir Frederick Pollock, 1906), chap. 8.

——— Early History of Institutions, 1874; American ed., 98–118.

——— Early Law and Custom, 1883; American ed. 1886, 335–361.

Duguit, Les Transformations générales du droit privé, 1912. Trans. in Continental Legal History Series, *11* (1918), chap. 3, 129–146.

Wagner, Volkswirtschaft und Recht, besonders Vermögensrecht, 1894.

Perreau, Cours d'économie politique (1916), Vol. *2*, §§ 623–695.

De la Grasserie, Les Principes sociologiques du droit civil (1906), chap. 3.

Fouillée, La Propriété sociale et la démocratie, 1884.

Landry, L'Utilité sociale de la propriété individuelle, 1901.

Meyer, L'Utilité publique et la propriété privée, 1893.

Thézard, La Propriété individuelle: Étude de philosophie historique du droit, 1872.

Thomas, L'Utilité publique et la propriété privée, 1904.

Berolzheimer, System der Rechts- und Wirtschaftsphilosophie, Vol. *4* (1907), §§ 1–13, philosophy of interests of substance.

Felix, Entwickelungsgeschichte des Eigenthums, 1883–99.

Karner, Die sociale Funktion der Rechtsinstitute, besonders des
    Eigenthums, 1904.
Conti, La proprietà fondiaria nel passato e nel presente, 1905.
Cosentini, Filosofia del diritto (1914), 250-279.
Fadda, Teoria della proprietà, 1907.
Labriola, Sul fondamento della proprietà privata, 1900.
Loria, La proprietà fondiaria e la questione sociale, 1897.
Piccione, Concetto positivo del diritto di proprietà, 1890.
Velardita, La proprietà secondo la sociologia, 1908.
Husserl, Der Rechtsgegenstand: Rechtslogische Studien zu einer
    Theorie des Eigenthums, 1933.
Grotius, De iure belli ac pacis (1625), ii, 3, 1-5; ii, 6, 1 and
    6, 14, § 1.
Pufendorf, De iure naturae et gentium (1672), iv, 4, §§ 2-6, 14.
Locke, On Government (1689), chap. 5.
Blackstone, Commentaries on the Laws of England, 2 (1766),
    3-10.
Kant, Metaphysische Anfangsgründe der Rechtslehre (2d ed.
    1798), §§ 1, 6-7, 8, 10, 18-21.
Hegel, Grundlinien der Philosophie des Rechts (1821), §§ 44,
    46, 49.
Lorimer, Institutes of Law (2d ed. 1880), 215 ff.

CHAPTER 6

Ely, Property and Contract in Their Relation to the Distribution
    of Wealth (1914), 2, 576-751.
Amos, Systematic View of the Science of Jurisprudence (1872),
    chap. 11.
Herkless, Jurisprudence (1901), chap. 12.
Kohler, Philosophy of Law, trans. by Albrecht (1914), 134-191.
De la Grasserie, Les Principes sociologiques du droit civil (1906),
    chap. 6.
Duguit, in Progress of the Law in the Nineteenth Century, Con-
    tinental Legal History Series, 11 (1918), 100-124.
Kant, Metaphysische Anfangsgründe der Rechtslehre (2d ed.
    1798), §§ 18-21.

Hegel, Grundlinien der Philosophie des Rechts (1821), §§ 71–81.

Fichte, Grundlage des Naturrechts (1796), §§ 18–20.

Williston, The Law of Contracts (revised ed. 1936), Vol. *1* §§ 99–104A.

Ames, The History of Assumpsit, 2 Harvard Law Rev. 1, 53 (1888).

—— Two Theories of Consideration, 12 Harvard Law Rev. 515 (1898); 13 Harvard Law Rev. 29 (1899).

Beale, Notes on Consideration, 17 Harvard Law Rev. 71 (1903).

Langdell, Mutual Promises as a Consideration for Each Other, 14 Harvard Law Rev. 496 (1902).

Pollock, Afterthoughts on Consideration, 17 Law Quarterly Rev. 415 (1901).

Hershey, Letters of Credit, 32 Harvard Law Rev. 1 (1918).

Lorenzen, Causa and Consideration in the Law of Contracts, 28 Yale Law Jour., 621 (1919).

Pound, Consideration in Equity, 13 Illinois Law Rev. 667, Celebration Legal Essays (1919), 435, essays in honor of John H. Wigmore.

Lord Wright, Ought the Doctrine of Consideration to be Abolished from the Common Law, 49 Harvard Law Rev. 1225 (1936).

Gardner, An Inquiry into the Principles of the Law of Contracts, 46 Harvard Law Rev. 1 (1927).

Pound, Interests of Substance—Promised Advantages, 59 Harvard Law Rev. 1 (1945).

Seavey, Reliance upon Gratuitous Promises or Other Conduct, 64 Harvard Law Rev. 913 (1951).

Cohen, Law and the Social Order (1933), chap. 2.

Llewellyn, What Price Contract?, 40 Yale Law Jour., 704 (1931).

Friedmann, Law and Social Change in Contemporary Britain (1951), 34–72.

Planiol, Traité élémentaire du droit civil, revised by Ripert and Boulanger (4 ed. 1952), Vol. *2*, §§ 443–480.

Josserand, Cours de droit civil postif français (3d ed. 1939), Vol. *2*, §§ 402–405.

Index

THE YALE PAPERBOUNDS